THE TRUE STORY

OF THE

Exodus of Israel

TOGETHER WITH A BRIEF VIEW OF

THE HISTORY OF MONUMENTAL EGYPT

COMPILED FROM THE WORK OF

DR. HENRY BRUGSCH-BEY

EDITED WITH AN INTRODUCTION
AND NOTES

BY FRANCIS H. UNDERWOOD

ISBN: 978-1-63923-607-7

All Rights reserved. No part of this book maybe reproduced without written permission from the publishers, except by a reviewer who may quote brief passages in a review to be printed in a newspaper or magazine.

Printed: January 2023

Published and Distributed By:
Lushena Books
607 Country Club Drive, Unit E
Bensenville, IL 60106
www.lushenabks.com

ISBN: 978-1-63923-607-7

CONTENTS.

	PAGE
INTRODUCTION,	9

CHAPTER I.
ORIGIN OF THE ANCIENT EGYPTIANS.—THEIR NEIGHBORS, 21

CHAPTER II.
DIVISION OF THE COUNTRY.—MENTAL PECULIARITIES OF THE EGYPTIANS, ... 28

CHAPTER III.
THE CHRONOLOGY OF THE PHARAONIC HISTORY, . . . 42

CHAPTER IV.
MENA, AND THE EARLY DYNASTIES.—THE PYRAMIDS AND SPHINX, ... 47

CHAPTER V.
ART AND ARCHITECTURE IN THE TWELFTH DYNASTY, . . 59

CHAPTER VI.
SEMITES AND THE EGYPTIANS, ... 64

CHAPTER VII.
THE TIME OF FOREIGN DOMINION.—JOSEPH IN EGYPT, . 95

CHAPTER VIII.
THE EIGHTEENTH DYNASTY. — THUTMES III., ... 139

CHAPTER IX.
AMENHOTEP III., AND KHUNATEN, THE HERETIC, . . . 153

CHAPTER X.
THE PHARAOH OF THE OPPRESSION, ... 168

CHAPTER XI.
THE PHARAOH OF THE EXODUS, AND A SUMMARY OF SUCCEEDING HISTORY, ... 183

CHAPTER XII.
THE EXODUS AND THE EGYPTIAN MONUMENTS. — A MEMOIR BY HENRY BRUGSCH-BEY, ... 196

APPENDIX.
THE TABLE OF ABYDUS, ... 243
OBELISKS OF THUTMES III. AT HELIOPOLIS, ... 248
NOTES, ... 253
INDEX, ... 257

INTRODUCTION.

"Egypt under the Pharaohs," by Dr. Henry Brugsch-Bey, is prominent among the ablest works upon the history and antiquities of the dead mother of arts. The author, under the patronage of the Egyptian government, spent thirty years in exploration and in the study of inscriptions, mostly in company with the distinguished French *savant*, Mons. Mariette-Bey, whose numerous discoveries have been fortunately complemented by the profound knowledge and the far-reaching deductions of his associate.

The most important fact established by their labors is the verification (in the main) of the chronological tables of Manetho, and the proof of the high antiquity of the kingdom. This antiquity, beside which the origin of every other historic nation is modern, is made clear by many independent proofs, sometimes jarring as against each other, but agreeing in general tendency. The Turin papyrus, an enormous list of pharaohs, unfortunately much dilapidated and illegible in places; the Table of Abydus, a smaller list of kings; a well-authenticated chart of genealogies of court architects; the various inscriptions upon temple walls; the portrait statues; and the cartouches of kings (like coats-of-arms) sculptured upon contemporary monuments, — these are the chief sources of the evidence which fixes the age of Mena, founder of the monarchy, between forty-four and fifty-seven centuries before the Christian era, and which shows a succession of pharaohs down to the time of Alexander the Great, (B. C. 332.) The architectural remains in Asia and in Central America may be older than the pyramids, but there are no inscriptions, and the date of Indian and of Aztec temples is wholly conjectural.

The antiquity of Egypt, however, is not its only claim upon the veneration of men: literature, the arts, and the ideas of morality and religion, so far as we know, had their birth in the Nile valley. The alphabet, if it was constructed in Phœnicia, was conceived in Egypt, or developed from Egyptian characters. Language, doubtless, is as old as man, but the visible symbols of speech were first formulated from the hieroglyphic figures.

The early architecture of the Greeks, the Doric, is a development of the Egyptian. Their vases, ewers, jewelry, and other ornamental works, are copied from the household luxury of the pharaohs. The peculiar genius of Egypt, however, appears to be repulsive to gay and lively people like the French, and the critics of Paris do scant justice to the colossal works of the elder pharaohs. Edmund About says: " The contemporaries of Sesostris were miraculous constructors rather than great architects, skilful and expeditious workmen rather than remarkable sculptors. From the time of Moses to the epoch of the Ptolemies, all the fine arts of the country, such as architecture, sculpture, and painting, have struck us by their solidity and harshness, by the spirit of tradition pushed to the extreme, rather than by their originality of genius. It is necessary to go back to the first dynasties to meet pure and ingenious talent, that hieratic regulations were soon to paralyze. A few specimens, well executed, are found here and there; but one could search the whole of Egypt from one end to the other, without finding a work to be compared to the Temple of Theseus, or to the Venus of Milo. The enormous is not the great; knowledge and facility bear no relation to genius."

There is a singular mixture of truth and error in this shrewd paragraph. 'Sesostris,' or Ramses the Great, was not long before Moses, but the art of Egypt culminated in the reign of Thutmes III., in the dynasty preceding. The art of the Greeks did not reach its perfection until long after the decadence of Egypt. In the time of the Ptolemies Egypt was a Greek province. The great works of Egypt, as About says, were not the latest; neither were they the earliest. The same is true of Greek and of Roman art. In no country has the growth of art been continuous and uninterrupted. In Egypt, as in Greece, the period of greatness was comparatively ancient. The most truthful statement in the passage quoted is that which mentions the influence of the priests in preventing the development of art in sculpture and painting, by requiring the use of certain formal and conventional outlines. After all, the appreciation of one or another kind of art is greatly owing to inherited traits, and to the distinctive quality of race. The exquisite perfection of a Greek temple will most delight the beauty-loving Latin races; the monumental grandeur of Karnac will most strongly affect the Germans, the English, and other Gothic peoples. It is the sombre magnificence of a Gothic minster against the tawdry splendors of the opera house; it is the glory of Handel's *Messiah*, or of Beethoven's *Fifth Symphony*, against the elegance of *La Dame Blanche*, or the gayety of *La Belle Hélène*, of Offenbach. Surely M. About can have his choice.

INTRODUCTION. 13

The influence of Egyptian. ideas upon the race of Israel has a profound interest for the whole Christian world. The time of Abraham is properly considered to have been about 1900 B. C.* — an epoch that, in the minds of unreflecting persons, is almost at the beginning of all things. Yet the Great Pyramid, built by the first pharaoh of the fourth dynasty, had been standing from twelve hundred to two thousand years before the 'Father of the Faithful' was born. Egypt had a school of architecture and sculpture, a recorded literature, religious ceremonies, mathematics, astronomy, music, agriculture, scientific irrigation, the arts of war, ships, commerce, workers in gold, ivory, gems, and glass, the appliances of luxury, and the insignia of pride, ages before the race of Hebrews had been evolved from the fierce Semitic tribes of the desert.

The Five Books of Moses, the beautiful poem of Job, and the other sacred writings of the Jews, were then so far in the future! Ages before the giving of the law on Mount Sinai, the 'Book of the Dead,' with its high moral precepts, was in the possession of every educated Egyptian; portions of

---

* The epoch of Abraham may be fixed by that of Joseph, who went to Egypt B. C. 1730. It is possible that from Joseph back to Abraham there might have been two hundred and ten years, allowing seventy years for each intervening life.

it, transcribed upon papyrus leaves, were even then, in the time of Abraham, securely folded in the funeral cerements of kings and priests, laid in their "everlasting habitations."

The prayers of King Khunaten and of his queen, and those of Amenhotep II., all dating long before any biblical writing, may be found translated in this work of Dr. Brugsch; and it is but simple truth to say, that, in beauty of expression and grandeur of thought, and in that piety which is the reaching out of the soul after God, no prayers of any people, under any form of religion, can be placed before them. One or two specimens will be found in the following pages.

We read with a vague awe when the sacred writer mentions "The God of Abraham, and of Isaac, and of Jacob;" but who was the God of Khunaten, whose cry to the deity he could not name comes to us from the dim twilight of time?

Other literary fragments, translated by Dr. Brugsch, attest the acute observation, the good sense, and the moral elevation of writers who preceded by centuries all others of every other race.

In this essay we leave out of view the civilization of Assyria and of other nations whose art and letters, so far as we know, have not greatly affected our own.

INTRODUCTION. 15

The people of modern Europe are heirs to the Romans in literature and the arts. The more northern of the nations inherit, also, the laws, language, and genius of the Goths. The Romans, with their allies and congeners, drew their ideas from the Greeks. The Greeks had their original learning and art from Egypt, though partly through the medium of Phœnicia. Greek historians like Herodotus, and philosophers like Pythagoras, went to Egypt to study, just as, long after, Roman scholars went to Athens. The Jews went out from Egypt with a modified Semitic speech, and a pure Semitic blood; but they carried with them in the person of their great leader "all the wisdom of the Egyptians." This is shown by their architecture, their religious customs and vestments, and their persistent kindred traditions. The nations we have mentioned are those that developed and taught the rude primitive races that peopled England, and whose descendants in all quarters of the globe are tending to supreme power in human affairs.

We see there is sufficient reason for the absorbing interest felt by all thoughtful men in the annals of Egypt. Wonderful developments have taken place since the greatest of the pharaohs wore the double crown, but the germ of all future civilizations was in that powerful people. The thinking and the living of all mankind have been moulded by the influences of Moses and Jesus; and both were of the race whose early lessons were received with stripes from Egyptian masters. The hieratic symbols are uncouth to modern eyes, but they contained the possibilities of Genesis and the Iliad, of the Psalms, the Æneid, and the Inferno, — of Prometheus, Hamlet, and Paradise Lost.

> "Earth proudly wears the Parthenon
> As the best gem upon her zone;"

but in the thought that planned the Hall of Columns, or sculptured the rock temple of Amon, was involved the conception of all Athenian and all Roman fanes.

We hail, therefore, the continued results of explorations in this wonderful land, the remote but undoubted source of letters and morals, sciences and arts. Every newly-found inscription helps to confirm or correct a date or a tradition, and to make certain the long and dim tract of its history.

The difficulties that have surrounded the delvers in buried cities can scarcely be over-estimated. Suppose that, by some convulsion of nature, or by some mischance in war, the venerable abbey of Westminster with its historic monuments had been levelled to the ground, and the stones lay in heaps in the cloisters, or about Whitehall, or along the Thames embankment;—suppose, after twenty centuries had covered these stones with their accumulations, and after spoliators had built some of them into modern edifices, that a new Mariette or Brugsch should excavate and measure and decipher, and should attempt to reconstruct the towers, nave, transepts, chapels, choir, and tombs;—think of the confusion of arches and rosaces, pinnacles and columns, of headless statues and overturned pedestals, of half-effaced inscriptions and fragmentary dates! Conceive what it would be to put in order the various parts of the building, and to identify its centuries of memorials! Such, and so broken and dispersed, are the remains of the fabric of the Egyptian state. So, through the Nile valley, and around Thebes and Memphis, Zoan-Tanis and Pitom, Thinis, Philæ, Bubastis and Abydus, lie the almost irrecoverable fragments of monumental Egypt, too many of them mere disjointed stones. Upon such materials the labors of Egyptologists have been patiently spent. The gaps in chronology are still enormous and deplorable, due to the numerous wars which, age after age, desolated the country and destroyed its statues and public buildings; but the results are still grand, and fully repay the toil and money spent in the search.

Much remains to be done; and it is to be hoped that future viceroys may be as intelligent and liberal as Ismail Pacha, to whom so much honor is due, and that future archæologists may be as untiring, as keen and as just, as the author whose work is under consideration.

This volume contains so much of Dr. Brugsch's work as relates to the settlement of the family of Jacob, and to their exodus as a people under Moses. To enable the reader to understand the historic connection, the editor has made a brief summary of leading events, and an account of the most eminent of the pharaohs. Some account is given of the early races, also of the royal residences, and of the Hyksos, under the last of whom Joseph was the favorite minister. As far as is consistent with fluency in narration, all these topics are presented in the author's own words.

The original work is large and expensive, and its chief interest to general readers, and especially to biblical students, lies in the contact of the Jewish with the Egyptian race. Many people might be indifferent as to the history of Ramses the Great, unless they knew that it was his daughter, the Princess Meri, who found the infant Moses. Aahmes would be a meaningless name, unless we knew that he overthrew and seated himself on the throne of the pharaoh who had been the patron of Joseph. Mineptah would be passed by, unless we were told that he was the pharaoh of the Exodus, upon whom the judgments of heaven fell, and who was drowned with his host in pursuing his slaves.

It will be interesting, even to the firmest believer in the literal inspiration of the Books of Moses, to know that, although Egyptian history is silent with regard to the Hebrews and their miraculous escape from bondage, the Scripture narrative, when rightly interpreted, is found to accord with known events and dates, and with the permanent facts of geography. Translators and commentators have darkened and perplexed the sacred record; and clerical chronologists have made havoc with arithmetic and with science and history in fixing the unknowable *anno mundi* as a point of reckoning; but in the new light shed upon the story of the Exodus by Dr. Brugsch it comes out with wonderful vividness.

The long sojourn of the Israelites in Egypt was productive of great and lasting results. Had they remained outside the barrier of Shur among the Shasu, their descendants to-day would have been like the Bedouins, dwellers in the black tents of the desert. Centuries of oppression consolidated them, and made them a hardy and warlike people. They learned the sciences and arts of their oppressors; they built upon their customs and laws. They came to have a proper pride in an unmixed lineage; and they carried into Syria the certainty of a one God, — a God long before dreamed of by Egyptian priests and kings. Other influences have doubtless aided, but it was chiefly the primal impulse from Egypt that made them a leading race; and that it has not yet spent its force is shown by their deserved prominence in literature, music, finance, and statesmanship. Familiar as the sacred story ought to be, it is thought best to copy the passages of scripture that refer to Joseph and to Moses, that they may be considered with Dr. Brugsch's irresistible demonstration.

FRANCIS H. UNDERWOOD.

BOSTON, Feb. 2, 1880.

THE TRUE STORY

OF

THE EXODUS OF ISRAEL.

CHAPTER I.

ORIGIN OF THE ANCIENT EGYPTIANS. — THEIR NEIGHBORS.

ALTHOUGH, in so long a space of time as sixty centuries, events and revolutions of great historical importance must of necessity have completely altered the political state of Egypt; yet, notwithstanding all, the old Egyptian race has undergone but little change; for it still preserves to this day those distinctive features of physiognomy, and those peculiarities of manners and customs, which have been handed down to us, by the united testimony of the monuments and the accounts of the ancient classical writers, as the hereditary characteristics of this people.

The forefathers of the Egyptians cannot be reckoned among the African races, properly so called. The form of the skull — so at least the elder school teaches — as well as the proportions of the several parts of the body, as these have been determined from examining a great number of mummies, are held to indicate a connection with the Caucasian family of mankind. The Egyptians, together with some other nations, form, as it would seem, a third branch of that race, namely, the family called Cushite, which is distinguished by special characters from the Pelasgian and the Semitic families. Whatever relations of kindred may be found always to exist between these great races of mankind, thus much may be regarded as certain, that the cradle of the Egyptian people must be sought in the interior of the Asiatic quarter of the world. In the earliest ages of humanity, far beyond all historical remembrance, the Egyptians, for reasons unknown to us, left the soil of their primeval home, took their way towards the setting sun, and finally crossed that bridge of nations, the Isthmus of Suez, to find a new fatherland on the favored banks of the holy Nile.

Comparative philology, in its turn, gives powerful support to this hypothesis. The Egyptian language — which has been preserved on the monuments of the oldest time, as well as in the late-Christian manuscripts of the Copts, the successors of the people of the pharaohs — shows in no way any trace of a derivation and descent from the African families of speech. On the contrary, the primitive roots and the essential elements of the Egyptian grammar point to such an intimate connection with the Indo-Germanic and Semitic languages, that it is almost impossible to mistake the close relations which formerly prevailed between the Egyptians and the races called Indo-Germanic and Semitic.

We will not pass over in silence a Greek account, remarkable because of its origin, according to which the primitive abode of the Egyptian people is to be sought in Ethiopia. According to an opinion strongly advocated by ancient writers, and even subscribed to by some modern historians little conversant with the facts of the case, the honor of first founding Egyptian civilization should be awarded to a society of priests from the city of Meroë. Descending the course of the Nile — so runs the story — they are supposed to have settled on the territory of the later city of Thebes, and there to have founded the first state with a theocratic form of government. Although, on the ground of the ancient tradition, this view has been frequently repeated in the historical works of subsequent times, it is nevertheless stamped with the mark of error, as it dispenses with any actual proof. It is not to the Ethiopian priests that the Egyptian empire owes its origin, its form of government, and the characteristic stages of its high civilization; but much rather was it the Egyptians that first ascended the river, to found in Ethiopia temples, cities, and fortified places, and to diffuse the blessings of a civilized state among the rude dark-colored population. Whichever of the Greek historians concocted the marvellous fiction of the first Ethiopic settlement in Egypt was led into the mistake by a confusion with the influence which Ethiopia exercised on the fortunes of Egypt during a comparatively late period, and by carrying this back, without further consideration, into the prehistoric age.

Supposing, for a moment, that Egypt had owed her civil and social development to Ethiopia, nothing should be more probable than the presumption of our finding monuments of the highest antiquity in that primitive home of the Egyptians, while in going down the river we ought to light only upon monuments of a later age. Strange to say, the whole number of the buildings in stone, as yet known and examined, which were erected on both sides of the river at the bidding of the Egyptian and Ethiopian kings, furnish the incontrovertible proof, that the long series of temples, cities, sepulchres, and monuments in general, exhibit a distinct chronological order, of which the oldest starting-point is found in the Pyramids, at the apex of the Delta, south of the bifurcation of the great river. As, in proceeding southwards, we approach nearer and nearer to the rapids and cataracts of the Upper Nile, right into the heart of the later Ethiopian kingdom, the more does the stamp of antiquity vanish from the whole body of extant monuments; the more evident is the decline of art, of taste, and of beauty. In short, the Ethiopian style of art — so far as the monuments still preserved allow us to form a judgment — is destitute of all independent character. The first view of the Ethiopian monuments at once carries the conviction, that we can recognize no special quality beyond the rudest conception and the most imperfect execution of a style of art originally Egyptian. The most clumsy imitation of Egyptian attainments in all that relates to science and the arts, appears as the acmé of the intellectual progress and the artistic development of Ethiopia.

According to the accounts of the Greek and Roman writers who had occasion to visit Egypt and to have close intercourse with the people of the country, the Egyptians themselves held the belief, that they were the original inhabitants of the land. The fertile valley of the Nile, according to their opinion, formed the heart and centre of the whole world.

To the west of it dwelt the groups of tribes which bore the general name of Ribu, or Libu, the aucestors of those Libyans who are so often mentioned in the historical works and geographical descriptions of the ancients. Inhabiting the north coasts of Africa, they extended their abodes eastward as far as the districts along the Canopic branch of the Nile, now called that of Rosetta, or Rashid. From the evidence of the monuments, they belonged to a light-colored race, with blue eyes and blond or red hair. According to the very remarkable researches of the French general Faidherbe, they may have been the earliest representatives of that race (perhaps of Celts?) who migrated from the north of Europe to Africa, making their way through the three Mediterranean peninsulas, and gradually taking possession of the Libyan coasts.

Turning our eyes to the east, across the narrow Isthmus of Suez, we meet on the ancient soil the people of that great nation, which the Egyptians designated by the name of Amu. Whether we prefer to explain this name by the help of the Semitic languages, in which it has the general significance of 'people,' or whether we resort to the Egyptian vocabulary, in which *ame* (more usually *amen*) has the meaning of 'herdsman,' — in either case, this one thing is certain, that the Egyptians of the pharaonic age used the term in a somewhat contemptuous sense. These Amu were the Pagans, the Kaffirs, or 'infidels' of their time. In the colored representations they are distinguished chiefly by their yellow or yellowish-brown complexion, while their dress has sometimes a great simplicity, but sometimes shows a taste for splendor and richness in the choiceness of the cut and the colored designs woven into the fabric. In these Amu scientific research has long since perceived the representatives of the great Semitic family of nations, though, in our own opinion, the same name includes also many peoples and families, who appear to have but a slight relationship with the pure Semitic race.

The most remarkable nations among the Amu, who appear in the course of Egyptian history as commanding respect by their character and their deeds, are the Kheta, the Khar (or Khal), and the Ruten (or Luten). But moreover it is to be especially remarked, as a fact established beyond dispute, that even in the most glorious times of the Egyptian monarchy the Amu were settled as permanent inhabitants in the neighborhood of the present lake Menzaleh. A great number of towns and villages, canals and pools, in that region, formerly bore names unmistakably Semitic.

CHAPTER II.

DIVISION OF THE COUNTRY. — MENTAL PECULIARITIES OF THE EGYPTIANS.

EGYPT is designated in the old inscriptions, as well as in the books of the later Christian Egyptians, by a word which signifies 'the black land,' and which is read in the Egyptian language Kem, or Kami. The ancients had early remarked that the cultivable land of Egypt was distinguished by its dark and almost black color, and certainly this peculiar color of their soil suggested to the old Egyptians the name of the black land. This name and its derivation receive a further corroboration from the fact, that the neighboring region of the Arabian desert bore the name of Tesher, or 'the red land,' in contradistinction to the black land (the A'in of the monuments, Æan in Pliny, an appellation of the nome afterwards called the Heroöpolitan). On countless occasions the king is mentioned in the inscriptions as 'the lord of the black country and of the red country,' in order to show that his rule extended over cultivated and uncultivated Egypt in the wider sense of the word. We must take this opportunity of stating that the Egyptians designated themselves simply as the people of the black land, and that the inscriptions, so far as we know, have handed down to us no other appellation as the distinctive name of the Egyptian people.

Ancient Egypt, most commonly mentioned in general as 'the double land,' consisted of two great divisions, which, after their situation, were called in contrast with each other the land of the South and the land of the North, as is attested by the inscriptions. The first corresponds to that part of Egypt which, following the Greek name, we now know as Upper Egypt, and which the Arabs of the present day call by the appellation of Said. The land of Upper Egypt began on the south at the ivory-island-city of Elephantine, which lay opposite to Syene (the modern trading-town of Assouan), on the right bank of the river; and its northern boundary reached to the neighborhood of the Memphian district on the left bank of the holy river. Northern Egypt comprehended the remaining part of the land, called the Low country, the land of Behereh of the Arabs, the Delta of the Greek writers. This division, which exists just as much in our own day as it did in the most ancient times, is neither accidental nor arbitrary; for it is founded not only on a local difference in the respective dialects of the inhabitants, but on the marked distinction of habits, manners, and customs, which divides the Egyptians in the north and the south from one another. Already in the thirteenth century before our era, this difference of speech is proved by documentary evidence.

The land of Egypt resembles a small narrow girdle, divided in the midst by a stream of water, and hemmed in on both sides by long chains of mountains. On the right side of the stream, to the east, the chain of hills called Arabian accompany the river for its whole length; on the opposite, the western side, the low hills of the Libyan desert extend in the same direction with the river from south to north, up to the shore of the Mediterranean Sea. The river itself was designated by the Greeks and Romans by the name of Neilos, or Nilus. Although this word is still retained in the Arabic language as Nil, with the special meaning of 'inundation,' yet its origin is not to be sought in the old Egyptian language; but, as has been lately suggested with great probability, it is to be derived from the Semitic word Nahar, or Nahal, which has the general signification of 'river.' From its bifurcation south of the ancient city of

Memphis, the river divided itself into three great arms, which watered the Lower Egyptian flat lands which spread out in the shape of the Greek letter Δ (Delta), and with four smaller arms formed the seven famous mouths of the Nile.

The Egyptian districts, called by the Greeks Nomes (Νόμοι), which in the upper land lay on both sides of the river, comprehended in the inner part of the Delta larger circuits, which were surrounded like islands by the arms of the Nile and their canals. Beyond these island nomes other districts extended on the Arabian and Libyan sides of the Lower Egyptian region of the stream. They are called in the lists the Western and Eastern nomes. This special division of the upper and lower countries into the districts called Nomes is of the highest antiquity, since we already find on the monuments of the fourth dynasty some nomes mentioned by their names, as well as some towns with the nomes to which they belonged. Upper Egypt contained twenty-two nomes, Lower Egypt twenty, so that there was a total for all Egypt of forty-two nomes.

Each district had its own capital, which was at the same time the seat of the captain for the time being, whose office and dignity passed by inheritance, according to the old Egyptian laws, from the father to the eldest grandson on the mother's side. The capital formed likewise the central point of the particular divine worship of the district which belonged to it. The sacred lists of the nomes have handed down to us the names of the temple of the chief deity, of the priests and priestesses, of the holy trees, and also the names of the town-harbor of the holy canal, the cultivated land and the land which was only fruitful during the inundation, and much other information, in such completeness that we are in a position, from the indications contained in these lists, to form the most exact picture of each Egyptian nome in all its details, almost without any gaps.

There are three districts, above all others, which in the course of Egyptian history maintained the brilliant reputation of being the seats of government for the land: in Lower Egypt the nomes of Memphis and Heliopolis (On), and in Upper Egypt that of Thebes.

The old inhabitants of Egypt, like their descendants of to-day who inhabit the 'black country,' obtained nourishment and increase from their favored soil. The wealth and prosperity of the country and its inhabitants were founded on agriculture and the breeding of cattle. Tillage, favored by the proverbial fertility of the soil, had its fixed seasons regulated by the annual inundations. The special care already bestowed in the remotest antiquity on that important part of agricultural industry, the breeding and tending of cattle, is set in the clearest light by the evidence of the monuments. The walls of the sepulchral chapels are covered with thousands of bas-reliefs and their explanatory inscriptions, which preserve for us the most abundant disclosures respecting the labors of the field and the rearing of cattle, as practised by the old Egyptians. In them, also, navigation plays an important part, as the sole means of transport for long distances. In ancient times, as in our own day, commerce and travelling were carried on upon the Nile and its canals. On the chief festivals of the Egyptian year the pharaohs themselves did not disdain to sail along the sacred river in the gorgeous royal ship, in order to perform mystic rites in special honor of agriculture. The priests regarded the plough as a most sacred implement, and their faith held that the highest happiness of man, after the completion of his pilgrimage here below, would consist in tilling the Elysian fields of the subterranean god Osiris, in feeding and tending his cattle, and navigating the breezy water of the other world in slender skiffs. The husbandman, the shepherd, and the boatman, were in fact the first founders of the gentle manners — the honored authors of that most ancient peaceful life — of the people who flourished in the blessed valley of the Nile.

We cannot close this chapter without still taking an inquiring look at the peculiar mental endowments of the ancient Egyptians, about which the information of the monuments will be of course our faithful guides. There are not wanting very learned and intelligent persons — not excepting some who have won an illustrious name in historical inquiries — who teach us to regard the Egyptians as a people reflective, serious, and reserved, very religious, occupied only with the other world, and caring nothing or very little about this lower life; just as if they had been the Trappists of antiquity. But could it have been possible — we ask with wonder and bewilderment — that the fertile and bounteous land, that the noble river which waters its soil, that the pure and smiling heaven, that the beaming sun of Egypt, could have produced a people of living mummies and of sad philosophers, a people who only regarded this life as a burden to be thrown off as soon as possible? No! Travel through the land of the old pharaohs; look at the pictures carved or painted on the walls of the sepulchral chapels; read the words cut in stone or written with black ink on the fragile papyrus; and you will soon be obliged to form another judgment on the Egyptian philosophers. No people could be gayer, more lively, of more childlike simplicity, than those old Egyptians, who loved life with all their heart, and found the deepest joy in their very existence. Far from longing for death, they addressed to the host of the holy gods the prayer to preserve and lengthen life, if possible, to the 'most perfect old age of one hundred and ten years.' They gave themselves up to the pleasures of a merry life. The song, and dance, and flowing cup, cheerful excursions to the meadows and the papyrus marshes — to hunt with bow and arrow or sling, or to fish with spear and hook — heightened the enjoyment of life, and were the recreations of the nobler classes after work was done. In connection with this merry disposition, humorous jests and lively sallies of wit, often passing the bounds of decorum, characterized the people from age to age. They were fond of biting jests and smart innuendos; and free social talk found its way even into the silent chambers of the tomb. But the propensity to pleasure was a dangerous trap for the youth of the old Egyptian schools, and the judicious teachers had much need to keep a curb on the young people. If admonition utterly failed, the chastising stick came into play, for the sages of the country believed that 'The ears of a youth are on his back.'

The lowest classes of the people, 'the mob,' as the inscriptions call them, were occupied with husbandry, the breeding of cattle, navigation, fishing, and the different branches of the most simple industries. From a very early period stone was wrought according to the rules of an advanced skill; and metals, namely, gold, silver, copper, iron (at first meteoric iron), were melted and wrought into works of art, or tools and implements; wood and leather were formed into a great variety of valuable objects; glass was cast; flax was spun and woven into stuffs; ropes were twisted; baskets and mats of rushes were plaited; and on the round potter's wheel great and small vessels were formed by clever artists from the rich clay of the Nile, and baked in the fiery furnace. Sculptors and painters found profitable work among the rich patrons of art at the court of the pharaohs; and a whole world of busy artisans worked for daily wages under the bright blue sky of Egypt.

But all these, the humble followers of the earliest human art industry, were held 'in bad odor,' and the lowest scribe in the service of a great man looked down with the greatest contempt on the toiling, laboring people. It was esteemed better to be a servant in the house of the pharaoh, and to bustle about in the service of their masters in the halls of the noble families. Though themselves children of the people, the class of servants found help and protection from their lords, and had a share in the honor of the court. Spoiled by the plenty, luxury, and extravagance of splendid life, they knew not the painful lot of the workman. Death itself did not grudge the servants a part with the owners of the gorgeous sepulchres; for in the chambers of the dead, the deep pits of which hid in the place of honor the embalmed bodies of the noble masters, room was reserved by the artist's hand for the memory of the faithful servant. But too obedient to the orders of their lords, the servants held in slight regard the 'stinking' masses of the people, and abhorred the society of the 'miserable' traders and workmen.

Returning from successful campaigns abroad to the banks of the holy river, the princes and captains of the warriors, in the course of time, brought a great number of prisoners into the country, as booty of war: king's children, nobles, and common people of foreign origin. Some as hostages, others as slaves, inhabited the towns of their Egyptian lords; those not noble being promoted to the rank of domestic servants, or condemned to work in the fields with the common herd of the people. Dark-colored inhabitants of the southern regions of the Upper Nile, and light-colored Canaanites, armed with sticks, attended the great men on their journeys as guards of honor, or, in the service of the court, enforced respect in an office like that of the cawasses of our day.

The noble class of the Egyptian people had nothing in common with the vulgar 'mob;' for they derived their origin, for the most part, from the royal house, the nearest branches of which, the king's children and grandchildren (Sutenrekh), were held in high honor and respect. To them were committed the highest offices of the court, to which they were attached by abundant rewards from the pharaoh's ever open hand. The nobles held as their hereditary possessions villages and tracts of land, with the people thereto belonging, bands of servants, and numerous herds of cattle. To their memory, after their decease, were dedicated those splendid tombs, the remains of which, on the raised plain of the Libyan desert, or in the caverns of the Egyptian hills, are still searched with admiring wonder by later ages down to our own day. Ambitiou and arrogant pride form a remarkable feature in the spirit of the old dwellers on the Nile. Workman competed with workman, husbandman with husbandman, official with official, to outvie his fellow, and to appropriate the favor and praises of the noble lords. In the schools, where the poor scribe's child sat on the same bench beside the offspring of the rich, to be trained in discipline and wise learning, the masters knew how by timely words to goad on the lagging diligence of the ambitious scholars, by holding out to them the future reward which awaited youths skilled in knowledge and letters. Thus the slumbering spark of self-esteem was stirred to a flame in the youthful breast, and emulation was stimulated among the boys. The clever son of the poor man, too, might hope by his knowledge to climb the ladder of the higher offices; for neither his birth nor position in life raised any barrier, if only the youth's mental power justified fair hopes for the future. In this sense, the restraints of caste did not exist, and neither descent nor family hampered the rising career of the clever. Many a monument consecrated to the memory of some nobleman gone to his long home, who during life had held high rank at the court of the pharaoh, is decorated with the simple but laudatory inscription, 'His ancestors were unknown people.'

It is a satisfaction to avow that the training and instruction of the young interested the Egyptians in the highest degree; for they fully recognized in this the sole means of elevating their national life, and of fulfilling the high civilizing mission which Providence seemed to have placed in their hands. But above all things they regarded justice, and virtue had the highest price in their eyes. The law which ordered them 'to pray to the gods, to honor the dead, to give bread to the hungry, water to the thirsty, clothing to the naked,' reveals to us one of the finest qualities of the old Egyptian character — pity towards the unfortunate. The forty-two commandments of the Egyptian religion, which are contained in the one hundred and twenty-fifth chapter of the 'Book of the Dead,' are in no way inferior to the precepts of Christianity; and, in reading the old Egyptian inscriptions concerning morality and the fear of God, we are tempted to believe that the Jewish lawgiver Moses modelled his teachings on the patterns given by the old Egyptian sages.

But the medal has its reverse side. The forefathers of the Egyptians were not free from vices and failings, which we cannot pass over in silence without exposing ourselves to the reproach of flattery at the expense of truth. Hatred, envy, cunning, intrigue, combined with an overweening sentiment of pride, opposition, and perversity, added to avarice and cruelty — such is the long series of hereditary faults which history reveals to us among the Egyptians by unnumbered examples in the course of centuries. We must especially beware of cherishing the belief that the rule of the pharaohs opened to the inhabitants of the land the gates of a terrestrial paradise. The people suffered and endured under the blows of their oppressors, and the stick settled the dispatch of business between the peasant and the tax-gatherer. We need but glance at the gigantic masses of the pyramids; they tell more emphatically than living speech or written words of the tears and the pains, the sufferings and miseries, of a whole population, which was condemned to erect these everlasting monuments of pharaonic vanity. Three thousand years were not able to efface the curse resting on their memory. When Herodotus, about the middle of the fifth century before Christ, visited the field of the great pyramids of Gizeh, the Egyptians told him of the imprecations wrung from their unhappy forefathers, and they would not, from abhorrence, so much as utter the names of the kings who constructed the two highest pyramids, whom we now know to have been the pharaohs Khufu and Khafra.

CHAPTER III.

THE CHRONOLOGY OF THE PHARAONIC HISTORY.

IF the reader's curiosity leads him to an inquiry concerning the epochs of time already fixed in the history of the pharaohs, and to a critical examination of the chronological tables thus far composed by scholars, he must be strangely impressed by the conflict of most diverse views in the computations of the most modern school. As to the era, for example, when the first pharaoh, Mena, mounted the throne, the German Egyptologers have attempted to fix it at the following epochs:

	B. C.		B. C.
Boeckh,	5702	Lauth,	4157
Unger,	5613	Lepsius,	3892
Brugsch,	4455	Bunsen,	3623

The calculations in question are based on the extracts that have been preserved from a work by the Egyptian priest Manetho on the history of Egypt. That learned man had then at his command the annals of his country's history, which were preserved in the temples, and from them, the best and most accurate sources, he derived the materials for his work, composed in the Greek language, on the history of the ancient Egyptian dynasties. His book, which is now lost, contained a general review of the kings of the land, divided into thirty dynasties, arranged in the order of their names, with the lengths of their reigns, and the total duration of each dynasty. Though this invaluable work was little known and certainly but little regarded by the historians of the old classical age, large extracts were made from it by some of the ecclesiastical writers. In process of time the copyists, either by error or designedly, corrupted the names and the numbers, and thus we only possess at the present day the ruins instead of the complete building. The truth of the original, and the authenticity of his sources, was first proved by the deciphering of the Egyptian writing. And thus the Manethonian list of the kings served, and still serves, as a guide for assigning to the royal names read on the monuments their place in the dynasties, as, on the other hand, the monuments have enabled us with certainty to restore to their correct orthography many of the kings' names which have been corrupted in the Manethonian lists. The very thorough investigations, to which learned experts have subjected the succession of the pharaohs and the chronological order of the dynasties, have shown the absolute necessity of supposing in the list of Manetho contemporary and collateral dynasties, and thus of diminishing considerably the total duration of the thirty dynasties. Notwithstanding all these discoveries, the figures are in a deplorable state. From the nature of the calculation, based on the exact determination of the regnal years of the kings, every number which is rectified necessarily changes the results of the whole series of numbers. It is only from the beginning of the twenty-sixth dynasty that the chronology is founded on data which leave little to be desired as to their exactitude.

Assuming, according to the well-known calculation of the father of history, Herodotus, the round number of a century for three consecutive human lives, we possess a means of determining approximately the periods of time which have elapsed, on the one hand, from king Mena to the end of the twelfth dynasty, and again from the beginning of the eighteenth dynasty to the end of the twenty-sixth.

The new Table of Abydus, discovered eleven years ago in a corridor of the temple of Seti I., at Harabat-el-Madfouneh, gives a succession of sixty-five kings from Mena, the founder of the line, down

THE EXODUS OF ISRAEL. 45

to the last reign of the twelfth dynasty. To these sovereigns therefore would be assigned a period of $\frac{65}{3} \times 100 = 2166$ years, leaving the fractional remainder out of the account.

If we were to believe the Table of Abydus alone, the princes of the twelfth dynasty would have had the pharaohs of the eighteenth dynasty for their immediate successors, without any break or interregnum. This would be in accordance with the fact perceived by the acuteness of Mariette-Bey, that the old Egyptian proper names of the persons of the twelfth, and especially of the eleventh dynasty, recur in the same forms on the monuments of the commencement of the eighteenth dynasty; and further, that at these two periods of Egyptian history the form and ornaments of the coffins are so alike as to be undistinguishable. Here we have a remarkable enigma, for the solution of which we do not yet possess the requisite data.

If we admit, according to the evidence of the Table of Abydus, the sudden transition from the twelfth to the eighteenth dynasty, the historical beginning of the Egyptian empire would fall about the year 3724 B. C., namely, two thousand one hundred and sixty-six years before 1558 B. C. But if, on the other hand, we assume in round numbers five hundred years as the intermediate space of time which divides the end of the twelfth from the beginning of the eighteenth dynasty, the result would be that Mena ascended the throne of Horus five hundred years before the year 3724, that is, in 4244 B. C.

Had the Turin papyrus been preserved to us in its entire state; had we possessed the complete list of the historical kings of the Egyptian empire, we should probably have been in a position to mould into a perfect shape even the most ancient part of Egyptian history, with the dates belonging to it. But, as the case stands at present, no mortal man possesses the means of removing the difficulties which are inseparable from the attempt to restore the original list of kings from the fragments of the Turin papyrus.

The chronological table of the history of the Egyptian kingdom, which is given at the end of this work (Appendix A), is founded on the principles above explained, as far as dates are concerned, and is only presented to the reader with the extremest caution. I would make the general remark, that the numbers of years assigned to the dynasties and to the individual pharaohs claim merely the value of an approximation, but nevertheless they do not on the average exceed their actual ages obtained from the monuments.

CHAPTER IV.

MENA, AND THE EARLY DYNASTIES. — THE PYRAMIDS AND SPHINX.

MENA, the founder of the monarchy, whose name signifies 'the constant,' reigned first at Tini, a little town of which scarce a trace now remains. According to tradition, he also built the larger capital of Memphis, having first made a site for the city by turning the course of the Nile. The Egyptian name is Mennofer, 'the good place.' The ruins of this city were well preserved down to the thirteenth century, at which time they were described in glowing phrases by an Arabian physician, Abdul-Latif. But the stones were transported to Cairo and used for the construction of mosques and palaces. This city, next to Thebes, holds a large place in Egyptian history. It was the first great seat of power, and for a long time the religious metropolis. Along the far-stretching margin of the desert, from Abu-Roash to Meidum, lay in silent tranquillity the necropolis of Memphis with its wealth of tombs, overlooked by the stupendous buildings of the pyramids, which rose high above the monuments of the noblest among the noble families, who, even after life was done, reposed in deep pits at the feet of their lords and masters. The contemporaries of the third, fourth, and fifth dynasties are here buried; but their memory has been preserved by pictures and writings on the walls of the sacrificial chambers built over their tombs. From this source flows the stream of tradition which carries us back to the time and to the soil of the oldest kingdom in the land. If this countless number of tombs had been preserved to us, it would have been an easy task to reconstruct before our eyes, in uninterrupted succession, the genealogy of the kings and of the noble lines related to them. Fate, however, has not granted this; for their monuments, names, and deeds are buried and forgotten; but even the few remaining heaps of ruins enable us to imagine the lost in all its greatness.

The eloquent language of the stones, speaking to us from the tombs of the necropolis of Memphis, tells us much concerning the usages of pharaoh and his court. The king himself is officially designated by the most complete title, 'king of Upper and Lower Egypt.' His high dignity is also concealed under other names, as, for instance, Perao — that is, 'of the great house,' well known as Pharaoh in the Bible. For his subjects the pharaoh was a god (nuter) and lord (neb) par excellence. At sight of him they were obliged to prostrate themselves, rubbing the ground with their noses; sometimes, by the gracious order of the king, they only touched the knee of the omnipotent. In speaking of him, they very often used the words 'his holiness.'

The royal court was composed of the nobility of the country, and of the servants of inferior rank. Not only the splendor of their origin gave the nobles dignity in the eyes of the people, but still more their wisdom, manners, and virtues. The persons belonging to the first class of the nobility generally bore the title Erpa, 'hereditary highness;' Ha, 'prince;' Set, 'the illustrious;' Semer-ua-t, 'the intimate friend.' The affairs of the court and of the administration of the country were conducted by 'the chiefs' or the secretaries, and by a numerous class of scribes.

The first king of whom much is really known is Senoferu, 'he who makes good;' his predecessors are shadows; he is an undoubtedly historic man.

So far as we are acquainted with the monuments, king Senoferu is the first ruler who had four titles of honor. Three name him commonly without difference 'the lord of truth;' the fourth is the name Senoferu, by which he was known to his father and his people. On the steep rock of Wody-Magharah, where ancient caverns have been formed by the hand of man, and the traces of the miners are easily discovered, Senoferu appears as a warrior, who strikes to the ground a vanquished enemy with a mighty club. The inscription, engraved by the side of the picture, mentions him clearly by name and with the title of 'vanquisher of foreign peoples' who in his time inhabited the cavernous valleys of the mountains round Sinai.

Even at this day the pilgrim, whom the desire of knowledge brings to these parts, and whose foot treads hurriedly the gloomy, barren valleys of Sinai, sees traces of the old works in the caverns dating from the spring-time of the world's history. He sees and reads on the half-worn stone a vast number of pictures and writings. Standing on the high rock, which boldly commands the entrance to Wady-Magharah, his eye discovers without trouble the last ruins of a strong fortress, whose stout walls once contained huts near a deep well, and protected the Egyptian troops from hostile attack.

The pharaohs of the fifth dynasty still resided at Memphis, and were the builders of the hugest of the pyramids.

According to the sure testimony of the tables of Abydus and Saqqarah, the successor of the

THE EXODUS OF ISRAEL. 51

good king Senoferu was Khufu. It is he whom the writers of Greek antiquity call sometimes Cheops (Herodotus), Chemmis or Chembes (Diodorus), while the epitomist of Manetho transcribes his name Suphis, and Eratosthenes, in the Theban list of kings, cites it as Saophis. With him begin the memorable traditions of Egyptian history.

No one who has had the happiness — whether from chance or purpose, or in the way of his calling — to set foot on the black soil of Egypt, ever turns back on his homeward way before his eyes have looked upon that wonder of antiquity, the threefold mass of the pyramids on the steep edge of the desert, which you reach after an hour's ride over the long causeway from the village of Gizeh, which stands close upon the left bank of the Nile. The desert's boundless sea of yellow sand — whose billows are piled up around the gigantic mass of the pyramids, deeply entombing the tomb itself, like a corpse long since deceased — surges hot and dry far up the green meadow, with its scattered vegetation where the grains of sand and corn are intermingled. From the far distance you see the giant forms of the pyramids, as if they were regularly crystallized mountains, which the ever-creating Nature has called forth from the mother soil of rock, to lift themselves up towards the blue vault of heaven. And yet they are but tombs, built by the hands of men, which, raised by king Khufu and two other pharaohs of the same family and dynasty, have been the admiration and astonishment alike of the ancient and modern world, as an incomparable work of power. Perfectly adjusted to the cardinal points of the horizon — the S. and N., the E. and W. — they differ in breadth and height, as is shown by the measurements of Colonel Vyse:

	Height.	Breadth at base.
1. Pyramid of Khufu,	450·75 feet.	746 feet (Eng.)
2. Pyramid of Khafra,	447·5 "	690 75 "
3. Pyramid of Menkara,	203 "	352·878 "

As soon as a pharaoh mounted the throne, the sovereign gave orders to a nobleman, the master of all the buildings of his land, to plan the work and cut the stone. The kernel of the future edifice was raised on the limestone soil of the desert, in the form of a small pyramid built in steps, of which the well-constructed and finished interior formed the king's eternal dwelling, with his stone sarcophagus lying on the rocky floor. Let us suppose that this first building was finished while the pharaoh still lived in the bright sunlight. A second covering was added, stone by stone, on the outside of the kernel; a third to this second; and to this even a fourth; and the mass of the giant building grew greater the longer the king enjoyed existence. And then, at last, when it became almost impossible to extend the area of the pyramid further, a casing of hard stone, polished like glass, and fitted accurately into the angles of the steps, covered the vast mass of the king's sepulchre, presenting a gigantic triangle on each of its four faces.

More than seventy such pyramids once rose on the margin of the desert, each telling of a king, of whom it was at once the tomb and monument. Had not the greater number of these sepulchres of the pharaohs been destroyed almost to the foundation, and had the names of the builders of those which still stand been accurately preserved, it would have been easy for the inquirer to prove and make clear by calculation what was originally, and of necessity, the proportion between the masses of the pyramids and the years of the reigns of their respective builders.

The Sphinx was sculptured at some time not far removed from the building of the three great pyramids. Recent discoveries have increased the astonishment of mankind at the huge bulk of this monstrous figure, and at the vast and unknown buildings that stood around it, and, as it were, lay between its paws. It is within a few years that the sand has been blown away and revealed these incomprehensible structures. In a well near by was found a finely executed statue of Khafra, builder of the second pyramid. Clear and significant inscriptions upon these temple-buildings attest the truth of tradition, and support the received chronology.

After Khafra's passage home to the realm of the dead, where the king of the gods, Osiris, held the sceptre, Men-kau-ra ascended the throne. His pyramid is called in the texts by the name of *hir*, that is, 'the high one.' When Colonel Vyse found his way to the middle of the chamber of the dead, and entered into the silent space of 'Eternity,' his eye discerned, as the last trace of Menkaura's place of burial, the wooden cover of the sarcophagus, and the stone coffin hewn out of one hard block, beautifully adorned outside in the style of a temple, according to the fashion of the masters of the old empire. The sarcophagus rests now at the bottom of the Mediterranean, the English vessel which was conveying it having been wrecked near Gibraltar. The cover, which was saved, thanks to the material of which it was composed, is now exhibited in the gallery of Egyptian antiquities in the British Museum. Its outside is adorned with a short text conceived in the following terms:

" O Osiris, who hast become king of Egypt, Menkaura living eternally, child of Olympus,* son of Urania, heir of Kronos, over thee may she stretch herself and cover thee, thy divine mother, Urania, in her name as mystery of heaven. May she grant that thou shouldest be like God, free from all evils, King Menkaura, living eternally."

This prayer is of very ancient origin, for there are examples of it found on the covers of sarcophagi belonging to the dynasties of the ancient empire. The sense of it is full of significance. Delivered from mortal matter, the soul of the defunct king passes through the immense space of heaven to unite itself with God, after having overcome the evil which opposed it during its life on its terrestrial journey.

The kings of the fifth dynasty continued to reside at Memphis, and each appears to have built a pyramid for his tomb, although but few of them can now be identified. The names, however, are preserved, such as Qebeh, 'the cool,' Nuter-setu, 'the most holy place,' and the like.

According to the monuments, the successor of Menkaura bore two names. The first, the most frequent, is Tat-ka-ra, and the second Assa. He has also left texts at Wady-Magharah, which tell us of works executed during his reign in the mines

* The translator here uses Greek equivalents that affect one like anachronisms.

of this mountain. His pyramid is called *nofer*, that
is, 'the beautiful;' unfortunately we have no means
of fixing its position. A very precious recollection
of him has been preserved in a literary work composed by his son, Prince Patah-hotep. Let us say
a word on this papyrus, which is probably the most
ancient manuscript in the world, and which is better known under the name of the Prisse papyrus.
It was bought by a Frenchman of this name at
Thebes, and given to the National Library at Paris.
The greater part of this document contains a
treatise by the son of Assa, and relates to the virtues necessary for man, and to the best manner
of arranging his life and making his way in the
world. The general title is conceived in these
words: "This is the teaching of the governor Patah-hotep under the majesty of King Assa; long may
he live." At the time when he composed his book,
he must have been very old, since he describes the
decrepitude of his old age in very significant terms.
"The eyes," he says, "are very diminutive, and the
ears stopped up; power is constantly diminished,
the mouth is silent and does not speak, the memory is closed and does not remember the past.
The bones are not in a state to render service;
that which was good is become bad. Even the
taste is gone. Old age makes a man miserable in

every way. The nose is stopped and does not breathe." It was thus that the prince begins the question which forms the subject of his book, which was to give to youth precepts which were justified by the practice of his long life, and frequently given in a humorous vein.

It is extremely interesting to follow the simple words which in an antique style represent the thoughts of the old man, and which touch almost all the conditions of human life. One of the most beautiful specimens is without doubt the following piece. He characterizes admirably the spirit of humanity which breathes through these precepts of a very high moral tendency. "If thou art become great, after thou hast been humble, and if thou hast amassed riches after poverty, being because of that the first in thy town; if thou art known for thy wealth, and art become a great lord, let not thy heart become proud because of thy riches, for it is God who is the author of them for thee. Despise not another who is as thou wast; be towards him as towards thy equal."

Although the tombs of this ancient epoch reveal to us frequently traits extremely favorable to our ideas of humanity, we cannot compare what they tell us with the naïve and simple language of the precepts of Prince Patah-hotep. It is neither the priest nor the prince who addresses the youth of his day; it is simply the man who teaches them. Nor is he a morose philosopher. Is there anything truer, and at the same time more persuasive, than his exhortation, "Let thy face be cheerful as long as thou livest; has any one come out of the coffin after having once entered it?"

CHAPTER V.

ART AND ARCHITECTURE IN THE TWELFTH DYNASTY.

WITH this fifth dynasty ended the first great division of the series of pharaohs, and also the pre-eminence of Memphis. The seat of government was transferred to middle Egypt, and at some time during the sixth dynasty Thebes arose. But though there are many pharaohs whose names are well known and of whose exploits there are some traces, yet for the most part a veil of impenetrable darkness rests upon the long period down to the end of the eleventh dynasty.

The twelfth dynasty stands out in a light that has almost the clearness of authentic history. It was a period in which strong monarchs ruled, and in which art was cultivated with magnificent results. Thebes was the capital, and upon its temples and palaces the most enormous labor and expense was lavishly bestowed. The sanctuary of the great temple of Amon, at Karnac, whose ruins present to us walls, columns (the so-called Proto-Doric), and pictures covered with the names of the kings of this house, kept on increasing from this time of its foundation, till it became an imperial building, whose walls of stone reveal to us the history of the Theban kings.

What lends a high worth to these ages is not only the greatness of the kings, founded on the wisdom of their domestic rule, and the glory of their victories in foreign countries: art also, with all its striving after beauty and noble forms, was cherished by these rulers, and skilful masters produced an immense number of beautiful works and pictures. Their ancestors of earlier times had already understood how to work with unknown but incomparable tools the hard substance of the granite and similar stones, to polish the surface like a mirror, and to fit the gigantic masses together, not unfrequently with iron clamps, as in the structure of the Great Pyramid. But, although the hand of the studious artist had worked in hard stone, and fashioned after life what nature had already produced in flesh and bone, yet there was still wanting the last stamp of perfection — namely, beauty which moves us to admiration. Beginning with the race of the Theban kings of the twelfth dynasty, the harmonious form of beauty united with truth and nobleness meets the eye of the beholder as well in buildings as in statues.

The great labyrinth and the excavation for the artificial lake Mœris were made during this period. In every part of the kingdom the power of these pharaohs was felt. In Tanis, 'the great city' of the lower country, inhabited all round by races of Semitic origin, the kings of the twelfth dynasty had already raised buildings and invoked the sculptor's art, to do honor to the gods themselves by these splendid works. 'The portrait of Usurtasen even has been found in some ruins of this temple world.

The rich paintings placed with profusion on the walls of the tomb of Khnumhotep, a great lord under the reign of Usurtasen II., have an inestimable value for a knowledge of the arts, the trades, and the domestic and public life of the Egyptians of this epoch, quite apart from the holy things to which, in detail, the paintings and inscriptions relate. The very interesting scenes with which the hall of sacrifice is adorned are of great importance in an historical point of view. They relate to the arrival in Egypt of a family of the Semitic nation of the Amu, which has quitted its native country to fix its abode on the blessed banks of the Nile. This family is composed of thirty-seven persons, men, women, and children, who present their respects to the person of Khnumhotep, asking of him, as it seems, a good reception. The royal scribe Nofer-hotep, an official in the service of Khnumhotep, offers to his chief a leaf of papyrus, with an inscription in this sense: "In the sixth year in the reign of King Usurtasen II.; an account of the Amu who brought to the king's son, Khnumhotep, while he was alive, the paint for the eyes called Mastemut of the country of Pitshu. Their number is composed of thirty-seven persons." The scribe in question is followed by another personage, an Egyptian by nation, whom a small hieroglyphic legend designates as 'the steward of those, of the name of Khiti.' Without doubt, then, these Semitic immigrants, as soon as they arrived in the territory of Khnumhotep, were placed under the care of Khiti. After these personages, who are charged with the introduction, the chief of the Amu presents himself with his suite. The first bears the name and the title of 'hak prince of the country of Abesha.' This name is of pure Semitic origin, and recalls that of Abishai, borne by the son of the sister of king David, who was distinguished by his military talents in the service of his uncle. Our Abesha approaches respectfully the person of Khnumhotep, whom 'the eldest son whom God had given him accompanies,' and offers him, as a gift or baksheesh, a magnificent wild goat of the kind still found in our day on the rocks of the peninsula of Sinai. Behind him we see his travelling companions, bearded men, armed with lances, bows, and clubs; the women, dressed in the lively fashions of the Amu; the children, and the asses, loaded with the baggage of the travellers, fixing their curious eyes on the Egyptian lord Khnumhotep; while a companion of the little party seems to elicit the harmony of sounds, by the aid of a plectrum, playing on a lyre of very old form. An inscription, traced above the scene which we have been describing, reads, 'paint for the eyes, Mastemut, which thirty-seven Amu bring.' The paint in question was an article very much prized in Egypt. It served as a cosmetic to dye the eyebrows and the eyelids a black color; and they painted under the two eyes a green stripe as a strange adornment. This paint was furnished by the Arabs or Shasu, who inhabited the land called Pitshu (the particular Egyptian term for the better known Midian), and, with their laden beasts, took the desert route from the east to Egypt, to traffic with the inhabitants of the Nile valley. This curious picture may serve as an illustration of the history of the sons of Jacob, who arrived in Egypt to implore the favor of Joseph. But it would be a singular error to suppose in this picture at Beni-Hassan any allusion to the history in the Holy Scriptures.

CHAPTER VI.

SEMITES AND EGYPTIANS.

ACCORDING to the testimony of the Turin book of the kings, the reigns of the rulers, who towards the end of the thirteenth dynasty occupied the throne, must have been of comparatively short duration, since they scarcely lasted on an average for four years. The cause of such a striking fact must be sought in internal troubles in the empire, in civil wars and struggles of individual occupants of the throne, who interrupted the regular succession, and made the existence of collateral dynasties very probable. Next to the kings of the thirteenth dynasty of Theban or Upper Egyptian origin, there appeared seventy-six pharaohs, who, according to the Manethonian account, had fixed their royal abode in the Lower Egyptian town Sakhau, or Khasan, called by the Greeks Xoïs. This internal discord, caused by the ambitious plans of the possessors of power in Upper and Lower Egypt, gives us on the one hand the explanation of the long silence of the contemporary monuments, and on the other hand a key to the full understanding of the success of the warlike invasion, which brought a foreign race into Egypt, who would never have dared to oppose the armed powers of the united empire of Kemi.

The inhabitants settled between the branches of the Nile were for the most part of pure Egyptian race. The boundary of demarcation, which separated this race from the neighboring peoples, was on the west the so-called Canopic branch of the Nile, as the Pelusiac branch was the boundary in the opposite direction to the east.

When we turn to the eastern boundary of the Delta, Semitism meets us according to the testimony of the monuments in the most evident manner. The principal region of it comprehends the country to the east of the Tanitic branch of the Nile, in which were situated the three Lower Egyptian nomes VIII., XIV., and XX. The capital of the fourteenth nome, the town of Tanis, which gave its name to the branch of the Nile which runs by it, bore the foreign designation Zar, Zal, and even in the plural Zaru, as if it were to be translated 'the town of Zar.' The name Tanis, which was given to it by the Greeks, is to be carried back to another designation of it, namely to the Egyptian form Zean, Zoan. It is the same name which we meet with in Holy Scripture as Zoan, which was built seven years later than Hebron; (Numbers xiii. 23.) The town of Tanis is everywhere in the Egyptian inscriptions designated as an essentially foreign town, the inhabitants of which are represented 'as the people in the eastern border lands.' The eastern border land is however nothing else than the ordinary designation of what was later the Tanaitic nome, which, although not often, appears in the list of nomes under the denomination of Ta mazor, that is, 'the fortified land,' in which may easily be recognized the long-sought most ancient form of the Hebrew name for Egypt, Mazor or Misraim.

On the granite memorial stone of the year 400, of the era of king Nubti, or Nub, which was discovered in Tanis, and whose designation of the year to this day puzzles the heads of the learned, there appears 'a governor of the fortress,' Zal, who besides this office enjoyed the title of 'governor of the foreign peoples.' In this example also there is question of inhabitants of foreign origin in that portion of the Egyptian Delta which we have mentioned.

The papyrus rolls of the time of the nineteenth dynasty with a certain preference busy themselves with this town, which, besides the two names we have mentioned, bore also a third, Pi-ramses, that is the 'town of Ramses.' About the origin of this name, and about the identity of the town Ramses with the biblical Ramses, we will further on collect together what is necessary to elucidate the subject. With reference to this question, the papyrus rolls to which we have alluded mention a number of lakes and waters, situated in the neighborhood of the foreign town Zal, whose peculiar designations at once remind us of their Semitic origin. I will mention as an example of the names of waters rich in fish and birds—the Shaanau, Putra, Nachal, Puharta or Puharat. The marshes and lakes rich in water-plants, which at this day are known by the name of Birket Menzaleh, were then called by the name common to all these waters, Sufi (or with the Egyptian article, Pa-sufi, which is the same as 'the Sufi'), which word completely agrees with the Hebrew Suf. The interpreters generally understand this word in the sense of rushes or a rushy country, while in old Egyptian it almost completely answers to a water rich in papyrus plants.

To the east of the Tanaitic nome, or the 'Eastern border land,' another nome was situated on the sandy banks of the Pelusiac branch of the Nile, the eighth in the general enumeration of the Egyptian nomes, which the inscriptions represent under the designation of the 'point of the east.' The capital of the nome we have mentioned bore the name Pi-tom, that is, 'the town of the sungod Tom,' in which we must immediately recognize the Pithom of the Bible. The town occupied a central situation of the district, whose name also must be referred to a foreign origin. It is the district Suko, or Sukot, the Succoth of the Holy Scriptures at the exodus of the children of Israel out of Egypt, the meaning of which, 'tent,' or 'tent camp,' can be only established by the help of the Semitic. Such a designation is not extraordinary for a district whose natural peculiarity quite answers to the meaning of the name, since it embraces places with meadows, the property of pharaoh, on which the wandering Bedouins of the eastern desert pitched their tents to afford necessary food for their cattle. Even as late as the Græco-Roman times of Egyptian history appears the designation 'tents;' and tent-camp (Scenæ) is also applied to places where they were accustomed to pitch their camp of tents. The site of the town Pitom is on the monuments frequently more closely defined by the important designation 'at the entrance of the east,' 'at the eastern entrance,' namely from the desert into Egypt. A piece of water in the neighborhood of the town received again a name borrowed not from the Egyptian, but Semitic language, namely, Charma, or Charoma, which means 'the piercing.'

To return once more to Sukot, we must remind the reader that the children of Israel in their journey out from the town Ramses pitched their first camp in the country called 'the tents.' On the second day they reached in their wanderings the place to which the Bible gives the name of Etham. I have elsewhere proved that this place also, according to Egyptian testimony, was either in the country of Sukot, or at least in its close neighborhood. It is the place called Chetam, on various occasions, in the hieratic papyrus rolls, the meaning of which, ' a shut-up place, fortress,' completely agrees with the Hebrew Etham. We shall have the opportunity of returning to this Chetam-Etham when we describe the exodus of the children of Israel.

In the same nome, the eighth of the description on the monuments, and the same which the Greeks and Romans used to call the Sethroitic, lay without doubt that most important town, which became the turning-point in the following history, the town Hauar, the literal interpretation of which is 'the house of the leg' (uar). In a particular place in the Manethonian description of the dominion of the foreigners, the so-called Hyksos kings, which has fortunately been preserved in an extract of the Jewish historian Josephus, there occurs a mention of the same name. Manetho names the town Auaris — and incidentally deduces its origin from a religious tradition. A closer examination of the nome with its towns, as they are described to us in the different more or less detailed and well-arranged lists on the monuments of the Ptolemies, renders it probable that other places also of the land of Egypt bore the name of Hauar, and particularly those which in their Serapeums, that is, in the temples of the dead, dedicated to the benefactor of the land, Osiris, carefully preserved the legs of the god as holy relics. Thus was named, for example, the capital of the third Lower Egyptian nome, or the Libyan, with a name added, Hauar-ament, that is, 'the town of the right leg.' The great inscription, so important for a knowledge of the land of Egypt, on the wall of the most holy place in the middle of the temple of Edfou (Apollinopolis Magna), completely confirms the statement that the inhabitants of that town of the Libyan nome, 'worshipped this leg in one of the temples dedicated to the Apis bull.' We may, therefore, with complete justice, maintain that the name also of the town Avaris, on the eastern side of the Delta, was connected with this peculiar worship of the leg of Osiris. Lastly, it is not difficult to recognize the left leg of the god, because of the evident reference to the peculiar situation of the arms of the Nile, which was well known to be considered as another form and manifestation of Osiris. After the stream has divided itself at the point of the Delta, into a fork in the neighborhood of a place called Kerkasorus (this designation seems to have the meaning of split, 'Kerk,' of Osiris), so as to form two main arms, or, as the Egyptians were accustomed to say, legs, the Canopic to the west, and the Pelusiac to the east, the western arm was considered as the right leg of Osiris, and the Pelusiac on the contrary as the left leg of the god. The towns situated in the neighborhood of the mouth were naturally considered as peculiar Osiris cities, in whose holy of holies the legs of that god played so peculiar a part. By this method of understanding it the saga finds its full explanation.

The town Hauar Avaris, with which we are at this moment occupied, lay, as we said, to the east of the Pelusiac branch of the Nile, with which, according to all probability, it was connected by a canal, if the theory should not be accepted that it was placed directly on the shore of the branch of the Nile at its mouth, when the river had become very broad. By a gradual silting up of this branch in the course of thousands of years, the restitution of the ancient bed of the river, and the right determination of the situation of the towns on its banks, has become so difficult a task, that we can have no hope of finding anywhere the site of the Hyksos town Avaris, which has disappeared, unless some very fortunate accident should bring about its discovery. But that Hauar must in any case be sought in the neighborhood of a lake is taught us in the most positive manner by the much cited inscription in the tomb at El-kab of the navigator Aahmes, the faithful servant of the pharaoh who, in the history of his life, relates how he came there, when the Egyptian fleet was engaged in fighting the foreign enemies in the waters Pa-zetku, or Zeku, of the town of Hanar. This name also, in spite of the Egyptian article placed before it, has a Semitic appearance, so that I should not hesitate to compare it with corresponding roots of Semitic languages.

Another place situated on the same territory of the Sethroite nome, bears on the monuments a purely Semitic name, Maktol, or Magdol; this is nothing else than the Hebrew Migdol, with the meaning of a 'town,' or fortress, out of which the Greeks formed on their side the well-sounding name Magdolon. That the ancient Egyptians were well acquainted with the meaning of this word, which was foreign to their language, is conclusively proved by the masculine article being placed before it, and the sign of a wall which was added to the foreign word when written in Egyptian. The site of this Migdol, of which mention is made in the Bible, not only in the description of the exodus of the Jews out of Egypt, but also in occasional passages, was distinctly stated to be at one of the most northern points of the inhabited country of the Egyptians; and as it also bore on the monuments the native name of Samut, must be sought in the heaps of rubbish at Tell-es-Samut on the eastern side of Lake Menzaleh. With this fortress Migdol, between which and the sea King Ramses III. once tarried with a portion of his infantry, as a not inactive witness of the victory of his Egyptian fleet over the confederated seafaring people of the islands and coasts of the Mediterranean, the list of defences, which were intended to protect the country on the east, is not yet closed. There lay in the direction of the north-east, on the western border of the so-called Lake Sirbonis, an important place for the defence of the frontier, called Anbu, that is 'the wall,' 'the circumvallation.' It is frequently mentioned by the ancients, not under its Egyptian appellation, but in the form of a translation. The Hebrews call it Shur, that is 'the wall,' and the Greeks ' to Gerrhon,' or ' ta

Gerrha,' which means 'the fences,' or 'enclosures.' This remark will at a stroke remove all difficulties which have hitherto existed with reference to the origin of this word, which in spite of difference in sound nevertheless refers to one and the same place.

Whoever travelled eastwards from Egypt to leave the country, was obliged to pass the place called 'the walls,' before he was allowed to enter the road of the Philistines, as it is called in Holy Writ, on his further journey. An Egyptian garrison, under the command of a captain, guarded the passage through the fortress, which only opened and closed on the suspicious wanderer if he was furnished with a permission from the royal authorities. Anbu-Shur-Gerrhon was also the first stopping-place on the great military road, which led from the Delta by Chetam-Etham and Migdol to the desert of Shur. From Anbu, passing by the fortress of Uit, in the land of Hazi, or Hazion (Kassiotis of the ancients), the traveller reached the tower, or Bechen, of Aanecht (Ostrakene), where occurred the boundary of the countries of Kemi and Zaha. On the foreign territory of the last-named place the traveller reached, always passing along the coast of the sea, the place Ab-sakabu (having the same meaning in Semitic as Rhinokolura, or Rhinokorura with the Greeks, namely, 'the place of the mutilation of the noses'), and at length reached the country of the inhabitants living on the borders of Palestine.

Thus there lay in the neighborhood of Mendes, perhaps even in Mendes itself, a fortified place called 'the fortress of Azaba,' the last part of which does not belong to the Egyptian tongue but to a Semitic stock. This is the fortress of Ozaeb, in Hebrew — i. e. 'of the idol.' Another well-known town, in the account of the war of the first Meneptah against the Libyan groups of peoples on the east side of the Delta, bore the appellation Pibailos, 'the town Bailos' (Greek, Byblos; Coptish, Phelbes), the Semitic origin of which is made clear by its evident relationship with the Hebrew, Balas (the mulberry). In its neighborhood was the lake Shakana, also with a non-Egyptian name, the meaning of which is only explained by the Semitic root shakan — 'to settle down, to live, to be neighbors to.' More inland, in the middle of the same region of the Delta, the traveller met, to the west of the Athribitic nome, the town Kahani, a name with a foreign Semitic sound, which recalls at once the Hebrew *kohen*, 'priests.' In this way it is not difficult by comparative philology to point out other examples of the connection between the names of Egyptian settlements and towns and ancient Semitic inhabitants.

But the presence of Semitic natives on the Egyptian land is shown from other sources, whether they were planted pure and unmixed on the soil, or were led by time and circumstances to seek their bread there. The memorial stones found in the cities of the dead in Ancient Egypt, and the coffins and the rolls of papyrus, show unmistakably the presence of Semitic persons, who were settled in the valley of the Nile, and had, so to speak, obtained the rights of citizenship; as also, on the other side, the inclination of the Egyptians to give to their children Semitic, or, by a singular mixture, half Egyptian and half Semitic names.

The inclination of the Egyptian mind to Semitic modes of life must, in my opinion, be explained from their having long lived together, and from very early existing mutual relations of the Egyptian and Semitic races. Above all things else, it must not be lost sight of that the trade relations, which extended from the Nile to the Euphrates, had contributed to introduce into Egypt foreign expressions for many products of the soil and foreign works of art. The animal world also, when they had not their home in the valley of the Nile, brought their contributions of words borrowed from the Semitic —

as, 'sus' for a horse, 'kamal' for a camel, 'abir' for a particular kind of ox. The endeavor to pay court, in the most open manner, to whatever was Semitic, became, in the time of the nineteenth and twentieth dynasties, a really absurd mania. They introduced Semitic words in place of Egyptian words already existing in their own mother-tongue, and in the writing of their country; and turned even Egyptian words into Semitic, by transposition of the syllables, if we may use such an expression. But the worst of it was that the most educated and best informed portion of the Egyptian people, the world of priests and scribes, found an especial pleasure in decking their history with Semitic words, which they used to employ in the place of good Egyptian expressions. They used Semitic expressions like the following: rosh, 'head'; sar, 'a king'; beit, 'a house'; bab, 'a door'; bir, 'a spring'; birkata, 'a lake'; ketem, 'gold'; shalom, 'to greet'; rom, 'to be high'; barak, 'to bless'; and many others.

We must here, on this subject, not forget a remark which, when well understood, is calculated to explain in some degree this striking fact, and to excuse what seems worthy of blame in this mania for the introduction of foreign words into the mother-tongue. In the east of the lowlands, in those countries of which we have spoken above, and whose central point was the cities of Ramses and Pitom, the Semitic immigration had extended so widely, and had reached such a preponderance over the Egyptian population, that, in the course of centuries, a gradual blending of both nations took place. It led to the formation of a mixed people, traces of which have been preserved unchanged in these places to the present day. The neighboring Egyptians, weaker in numbers, found it convenient not only to adopt the manners and usages of the Semites, but began to take an inclination to the worship of foreign idols, and to enrich their own divine lore with new and hitherto unknown heavenly forms of foreign origin. At the head of all stood, half Egyptian and half Semitic, the godhead of Set or Sutech, with the additional name Nub,* 'gold,' who was considered universally as the representative and king of the foreign deities in the land of Mazour. According to his essence, a most ancient Egyptian creation, Set, at the same time gradually became the representative of all foreign countries — the god of the foreigners.

* It is a very remarkable fact, that, from the times of the highest antiquity in Eastern representations, the curse of the Typhonic deities adheres to gold. According to a Greek tradition (Plutarch on *Isis and Osiris*, p. 30), at the sacrificial feast of Helios the worshippers of the god were directed to carry no gold about their persons, just as in the present day the followers of Mohammed take off all gold trinkets before they go through the appointed prayers.

If I mention the names of Baal and Astarta, which we so frequently meet with in the inscriptions, it is scarcely necessary to state that both have their origin in the Phœnician divine lore. As in Sidon, so in Memphis, the warlike Astarta (who in the Egyptian monuments of a later time was represented as a lion-headed goddess, guiding with her own hand her team of horses yoked to the chariot of war) had her own temple ; and we have proof that Ramses II. raised a particular temple to her honor and her service on the lonely shore of the Mediterranean, near the Lake Sirbonis.

Less frequently occurring on the monuments than the previously mentioned representatives of the Semitic divinities, the fierce Reshpu still had his place in the Egyptian host of heaven. He was called 'the end of long times, the king of eternity, the lord of strength in the midst of the host of gods;' and the goddess, Kadosh, that is 'the holy,' whose name already indicates the peculiar character of her heavenly existence. The frolicsome Bes, or Bas, also, the chief of song and of music, of pleasures, and all social amusements, must be mentioned in this place, since he was, according to his origin, a pure child of the Semitic race of the Arabs. His name, in their language, means Lynx and Cat; and we think we are not carrying the comparison too far if we at once place by his side the cat-headed goddess, the protectress of the town of Bubastus, the much venerated lissom Bast. If we also mention that the Phœnician Onka, and the Syrian Anait, or Anaitis, belong to those heavenly beings whose names and forms are again found in the Egyptian divine world, where they take their places under the names of Anka and Anta, then we have exhausted the principal representatives of the Semitic deities in the old Egyptian theology.

Perhaps the influence of the Semitic neighborhood on Egyptian matters might be proved from looking at it in a new point of view. In this case a very remarkable and striking fact will bear convincing evidence in favor of our views. We allude here to the peculiar era, found nowhere else, which an Egyptian courtier once used, in the fourteenth century before Christ, to indicate the year of the execution of an inscription. I refer to the celebrated memorial stone of Tanis, erected in the reign of the second Ramses.

Contrary to the custom and usage of reckoning time by the day, month, and year of the reigning king, the stone of Tanis offers us the only example as yet discovered, which, according to appearances, resorts to a foreign and not an Egyptian mode of reckoning time. There is here question of the year

400 of king Nub, a prince belonging to the foreign lords of the Hyksos. In other words, if we do not misunderstand the main issue, in the town of Tanis, whose inhabitants for the most part belonged to Semitic races, this mode of reckoning was in such general use that the person who raised the memorial-stone thought it nothing extraordinary to employ it as a mode of reckoning time in the beautifully engraved inscription on granite which was exhibited before all eyes in a temple. There can hardly be a stronger proof of the influence of Semitic manners on the Egyptian spirit and customs than the testimony we have brought forward of the stone of Tanis. A preponderating and almost irresistible power of Semitism lies hidden here, the importance of which it is as well to remark upon before we undertake to describe the history of the irruption of the foreigners into Egypt, and the consequences connected with it on the condition of the empire.

Taking into consideration all this testimony, which seems to speak in favor of our view of the importance of Semitic influence on Egyptian relations, we will question the monuments for confirmation of the presence of Semitic races and families on Egyptian soil. We will direct our attention to the eastern provinces of the Delta, which offered the only entrance to wanderers from the east.

As an answer, we insert the literal translation of a circular, which was composed in the course of the nineteenth dynasty, and with the view on the part of the writer to give a report to his superior on the admission of foreign immigrants to Egyptian soil.

"I will now pass to something else which will give satisfaction to the heart of my lord (namely to give him an account of it), that we have permitted the races of the Shasu of the land of Aduma (Edom) to pass through the fortress Chetam (Etham) of Mineptah-Hotephimaat — Life, weal, and health to him — which is situated in the land of Sukot near the lakes of the town Pitom of King Mineptah-Hotephimaat, which is situated in the land of Sukot, to nourish themselves and to nourish their cattle on the property of Pharaoh, who is a good sun for all nations."

In this extremely important document of the time of the first Mineptah, the son of Ramses II., there is question of the races of the sons of the desert, or to use the Egyptian name for these, the races of the Shasu, in which science has for a long time and with perfect certainty recognized the Bedouins of the highest antiquity. They inhabited the great desert between Egypt and the land of Canaan, and extended their wanderings sometimes as far as the river Euphrates. According to the monuments, the Shasu belonged to the great race of the Amu, of which they were the head representatives. In the times of the first Seti, the father of Ramses II., the land passed through by the Shasu began at the fortress Zal Tanis, and stretched towards the east as far as the hill-town 'of Canana,' in Wady Araba to the south of the Dead Sea, which Seti I. took by storm in his campaign against the Bedouins. The author of the writing designates those Shasu who were permitted by superior authority to enter the Egyptian kingdom, as the Shasu of the land of Aduma, which was the Edom of the Bible and the land of Idumæa of later times. The tribes of the Shasu, who are referred to in the circular we have quoted, were therefore sufficiently designated as inhabitants of the land of Edom. The position of these last is more closely defined in Holy Writ as the mountainous country of Seir.

On this occasion we have the satisfaction to declare once again the complete agreement of the information on the monuments with the statements of Holy Writ. In that place of the Harris papyrus, in which mention is made of the campaigns of king Ramses III. against these very Shasu, an important observation is introduced into the speech of the king. He speaks thus: 'ari-a sek Sair-u em mahaut Sasu;' that is, 'I annihilated the Sair among the tribes of the Shasu.' The name of Sair answers letter for letter with the Hebrew word Seir. The comparison must appear all the more founded, as the Egyptian writer has appended to the written words of the name the sign for dumbness, which is the hieroglyphic for a child, as if he wished by this to prove his knowledge of the Semitic language, in which Sa'ir means 'the little one.' The Se'irites, the children of Se'ir, were dwellers in caves, and original inhabitants of the mountain range of Se'ir. At a later period, hunted down by the children of Esau, they yielded their land to the conquerors, to whom the appellation of Se'irites, as inhabitants of the Se'ir range, was afterwards transferred.

With the help of this knowledge beforehand, it is no longer difficult to assign their true place to the Shasu on the theatre of events which are the object of our inquiry. The land of Edom and the neighboring hill-country was the home of the principal races of the Shasu, which in the fifteenth and sixteenth centuries before our era left their mountains to fall upon Egypt with weapons in their hands, or in a friendly manner followed by their flocks and herds to beg sustenance for themselves and their cattle, and to seek an entrance into the rich pastures of the land of Succoth. Manifestly the calls of hunger drove them to the rich corn lands of the

THE EXODUS OF ISRAEL. 85

blessed Delta, where they took up their abode in huts near their brethren of the same race, who had become settled inhabitants.

As in the neighborhood of the town of Ramses and the place Pitom the Semitic population had formed the main foundation of the inhabitants from hoar antiquity, and as subjects of the pharaoh had been obedient to the laws of the empire, so in the lapse of time, in another part of the eastern provinces, in the country of Pibailos (the Bilbeis of modern maps), close on the edge of the desert and in sight of the cultivated land, disagreeable neighbors had fixed themselves and pitched their tents where they found pasture for their cattle. These were Bedouins, who according to all probability found their way from the dreary desert through the difficult paths of the great papyrus marsh near the present town of Suez in a north-western direction, to find the object of their wandering near the town of Pibailos. Mineptah I., the son and successor of Ramses II., gives on the monument of his victories in Karnak a graphic account of the dangerous character of these unbidden guests to whom, from Pibailos to On and Memphis, the way lay open, without the kings his predecessors having found it worth while to establish fortresses, to bar the way of these strangers to the most important cities of the lower country. When the pharaoh we have named succeeded to the throne of his fathers, the danger of a sudden irruption on this side appeared all the more threatening, because on the other side the Libyans, the western neighbors of the Egyptians, with their allies suddenly passed the frontiers of Kemi, and extended their plundering raids into the heart of the inhabited and cultivated western nomes of the Delta. According to the report of the inscription of his victories (unfortunately injured by the lesion of the upper part), Mineptah I. saw himself obliged to take precautions for the safety of the land. For the protection of the eastern frontier, the capitals On and Memphis were provided with the necessary fortifications, for as the cited inscription expressly says, "the foreigners had pitched their *ahil** or tents before the town of Pibailos, and the districts at the lakes of Shakana to the north of the canal of the Heliopolite nome had remained unused, for they had been abandoned to serve as mere pasture of the herds because of the foreigners, and had become deserted from the time of our forefathers.† All the kings of Upper Egypt

---

* Again a Semitic word; the Hebrew *Ohil*, with the same meaning.

† The translation of this sentence presents a difficulty which I can hardly think I have solved. There can, however, be no doubt of the general meaning, and that the author of the inscription intended to say what I have pointed out in my translation.

were living in their magnificent buildings, and the kings of Lower Egypt enjoyed peace in their cities. All around the order of the land was threatened by disturbers. The armed force was wanting in people to assist them to give them an answer."

Before we cast a glance at the neighbors of the Egyptians of the Delta, who carried on war and traffic with the inhabitants of Kemi, it seems useful to attend to a particular circumstance, which is not without importance for arriving at a right judgment on Semitism.

Our advancing knowledge of the contents of the Egyptian papyri permits us, even at the present time, to cast an intelligent glance at the administration of the eastern provinces, which had for its central point the town of foreigners, Zoan-Tanis, in the time of the great Ramessides and their successors. Hence went forth the commands of the king, or of the chief officials of the king, relating to the management of business or the regulation of trade with ' the foreign nations,' or, to use the Egyptian expression for these, with the Pit. A portion of these consisted of the industrious settled population in towns and villages; another portion served in the army of the pharaoh as infantry and cavalry, or as sailors; others were used in the public works, the most laborious of which were the mines and quarries. Over each larger and smaller division of 'foreigners,' who with their names and origin were carried on the list of the royal archives, an official was placed, the so-called Hir-pit, or steward of the foreigners. His next superior was the captain of the district, or Adon (here also they used the Semitic form for this title), while as chief authority the Ab of the pharaoh (this was the dignity which Joseph held), or royal Wezer, issued orders in the name of the ruler. The authority over the foreign people lay in the hands of particular bailiffs (the so-called Mazai), who in the principal cities of the land had to look after and preserve public order, and who were under an Ur, or superior, by whom the carrying out of public buildings was frequently undertaken as an additional duty. I pass over a host of other officials, who, in the eastern provinces of the Delta as in the rest of Egypt, carried on the administration of the nomes, and I will only mention that frequently the foreign subjects were promoted to important offices in connection with the government. They seem to have been most appreciated as the bearers of official documents in the trade transactions between Egypt and the neighboring Palestine. The chief seats of this trade, the importance of which is shown by individual papyri, besides the frontier town of Ramses, seem to have been the fortified places near the Mediterranean sea-coast, and further inland to the east the country of the Edomites and Amorites.

We will embrace the opportunity we have long desired, in this place to consider the neighbors in Palestine, who continually carried on the most lively intercourse with the Egyptians in old time, and partially formed the foundation of the foreign inhabitants in the eastern provinces of the Delta. In the first rank stand the Char, or Chal, by which name not only a people but the country they inbahited was also known, namely, those parts of western Asia lying on the Syrian coast, and before all others the land of the Phœnicians. Richly laden ships went and came from the land of Char; for the inhabitants of Char carried on a lively trade with the Egyptians, and seem, if we are not to mistrust the monuments and the rolls of the books, to have been a highly-esteemed and respectable people.

Even the male and female slaves from Char were highly esteemed as merchandise, and were procured by distinguished Egyptians at a high price, whether for their own houses, or for service in the holy dwellings of the Egyptian gods.

The land of the Char bears in the inscriptions another name, the most ancient mention of which is supported by all the testimony we could desire, namely, by witnesses in the first times of the eighteenth dynasty, about the year 1700 B. C. It is always called Kefa, or Keft, Kefeth, Kefthu, on the monuments. As at a certain time of Egyptian history, namely, at the beginning of the reign of the first Seti, the territory of the Shasu extended as far as the town of Ramses, about a hundred years later, the seats of the people of Char, or the Phœnicians, were described as ' beginning with the fortress Zar (Tanis Ramses), and extending to Aupa, or Aup.' The last-mentioned name designates a place in the north of Palestine, without our being able more nearly to define its situation. On the other hand, the information is of very great importance, that these same Char had extended their seats quite into the heart of the Tanitic nome. We can, after the reasons we have given above, no longer be surprised that these descendants of Phœnician race constituted on the eastern frontier of the Egyptian empire the real kernel of its fixed, industrious, artistic, and before all, its sea-faring and commercial population. In their habits and mode of life they were directly opposed to those wandering Shasu, the children of Esau, who traversed the deserts, and only remained with their herds so long on the property of pharaoh as the pastures suited them and supplied sustenance for themselves and their cattle.

THE EXODUS OF ISRAEL. 91

The influence of the settled Char on Egyptian life is unmistakable in a thousand details, for a knowledge of which we have to thank the monuments, and particularly the little rolls of papyrus. Even the fortified town of Zoan, if we are not completely deceived, seems to have been a very ancient habitation of the Phœnicians, since as well on the water side of it as by land, Zoan-Tanis constituted at the entrance to the Delta on the east, an important emporium of intercourse and trade with the whole of the rest of Egypt. The name of the city Zor, used as well as that of Zoan, reminds us too much of the celebrated Zor-Tyrus in the native country of the Phœnicians, for us to leave it unnoticed in an account of the traces of the Phœnician race.

The presence of the Char-Phœnicians in Egypt is, as already observed, made known to us in the most detailed manner by the inscriptions. I have already before spoken of those Semitic inhabitants who were employed in Egypt in all sorts of official service. To these in the first line belong the Phœnicians, or Char. Their importance culminates in the fact newly communicated to us by the monuments, that a Char-Phœnician, towards the end of the nineteenth dynasty, was able to conquer the throne and dominion over the Egyptians.

The Char spoke their own language, the Phœnician, upon the peculiarities of which, in relation to the other Semitic languages, the Phœnician inscriptions that have been hitherto discovered have already preserved plentiful information. Of all the languages spoken by Arab and western Asiatic nations, the monuments only notice the language of the Char, with a clear reference to its importance as the most cultivated representative of all the others. Whoever lived in Egypt spoke Egyptian (the language of the people of Kemi); whoever stayed in the south was obliged to speak the language of the Nahesi, or dark-colored people; while those who went northwards to the Asiatic region must have been well acquainted with the language of the Phœnicians, in order in some degree to understand the inhabitants of the country.

The historical fact that the Phœnicians already, in the most ancient times of Egyptian history, formed a fixed settled population in the eastern provinces of the Egyptian empire, finds a kind of confirmation, or, if it is preferred, an explanation, from a remarkable circumstance. We mean the presence of the latest descendants of the old Phœnician race in the same seats which their forefathers occupied thousands of years ago. At this day the traveller meets on the shores of the Lake Menzaleh, near the old towns and districts of Ramses and Pitom, a peculiar race of fishermen and sailors, whose manners and customs, whose historical traditions, however weak they may be, and whose ideas on religious matters, prove them to have been strangers to the real Egyptians. The inhabitants of this country, formerly Christians, who call themselves by the name of Malakin, were restless and rebellious subjects of the Khalifs.

The same inhabitants of the eastern provinces, who at this day navigate in their barks the shallow waters of Lake Menzaleh, and carry on the fishery as their chief business, are, as has been said, the descendants of the Phœnician inhabitants of the Tanitic and Sethroitic nomes. These were the people who ages ago gave to the fortified places of their Egyptian lands, and to the towns and villages which they once inhabited, and to the lakes and canals on which they navigated, those Semitic appellations by which we well know these places from the papyrus rolls.

What most marks their ancient and now forgotten origin, is their non-Egyptian countenance, so like the pictures of the Hyksos, with broad cheek-bones, and with daring pouting lips, which more than anything else marks the boatmen of Lake Menzaleh with the stamp of a foreign origin.

The history of the inhabitants of the eastern provinces lies buried and forgotten under the rubbish heaps of thousands of years. And yet their fathers were once the lords of the fate of Egypt, before whose rough strength the pharaohs bowed themselves powerless, and were obliged for centuries to pass a furtive existence in the southern portions of the empire. Set had conquered Osiris.

CHAPTER VII.

THE TIME OF FOREIGN *DOMINION.*—JOSEPH IN EGYPT.

ACCORDING to the Manethonian account which the Jewish historian Josephus has preserved to us by transcribing it, the Egyptian Netherlands were at a certain time overspread by a wild and rough people, which came from the countries of the East, overcame the native kings who dwelt there, and took possession of the whole country, without finding any great opposition on the part of the Egyptians. The account of it in Josephus is literally as follows:—

" There was a king called Timaius (or Timaos, Timios). In his reign, I know not for what reason, God was unpropitious, and people of low origin from the country of the East suddenly attacked the land, of which they easily and without a struggle gained possession. They overthrew those who ruled there, burned down the cities, and laid waste the temples of the gods. They ill-treated all the inhabitants, for they killed some, and carried into captivity others, with their wives and children.

"And they made one from the midst of them king, whose name was Salatis (Saltis, Silitis). He fixed his seat in Memphis, collected the taxes from the upper and lower country, and placed garrisons in the most important places. But he particularly fortified the eastern boundary, for he foresaw that the Assyrians, then the most powerful people, would undertake to make an attack on his kingdom.

"When he had found a town very conveniently situated, in the Sethroite nome to the east of the Bubastic branch of the Nile — on the grounds of an old mythical legend — it was called Auaris — he extended it, fortified it with very strong walls, and placed in it as a garrison two hundred and forty thousand heavy armed troops.

"There he betook himself in summer, partly to watch over the distribution of provisions and the counting out their pay to his army, and partly also to strike fear into foreigners by making his army perform military manœuvres.

He died after he had reigned . .	19 years.
His successor, by name Bnon (or Banon, Beon), reigned	44 years.
After him another, Apachuan (or Apachnas)	36 years, 7 months.
After him Aphobis (or Aphophis, Apophis, Aphosis)	61 years.
And Annas (or Janias, Jannas, Anan) .	50 years, 1 month.
Last of all Asseth (or Aseth, Ases, Assis)	49 years, 2 months.

THE EXODUS OF ISRAEL. 97

" These six were the first kings. They carried on war uninterruptedly with a view to destroy the land of Egypt to the roots.

"The whole people bore the name of Hyksos, that is, 'shepherd kings.' For *hyk* means in the holy language a king, *sos* in the dialect of the people a shepherd or shepherds. These syllables, when put together, make the word Hyksos. Some think they were Arabs."

We will first of all turn our attention to the last statement, because it is of great importance for the fixing of the origin of this obscure people. If the kind reader will now recall to his thoughts what we have said about the Arab Bedouins, who inhabited the desert to the east of Egypt, and were called in Egyptian Shasu (also Shaus, Shauas), he will certainly be of the same opinion as ourselves, that those who maintain the Arab origin of the Hyksos, must have drawn their information from a pure Egyptian source. For that word Sos answers completely to the old Egyptian Shasu, in which the sound *sh*,*

---

* We will adduce further examples, borrowed from the work of Manetho, which leave no doubt that the Greek sign for *s* was used to represent the old Egyptian sound *sh*. Manetho transcribes the kings' names, Sheshonq as Sesonchis, Shabak as Sahakon, Shabatak as Sebichos. Also the name of king Chufu, which the Egyptians at the time of the composition of the work of Manetho which did not exist in Greek, according to usage was replaced by a simple *s*. Although Manetho, when he talks of the Hyksos, insists upon the meaning of shepherd, he could only do this in consequence of a strange confusion, since he turns to the new and popular language of his own time to explain the second syllable *sos*, in which accidentally *sos* (or *shos*, as the same word is still pronounced in Coptic) means a shepherd.

We have already before remarked how from time to time the Bedouin people of the Shasu knocked at the eastern frontier door to obtain an entrance into Egypt. We have, on the ground of testimony from an inscription of the time of the nineteenth dynasty, stated the certainty of their presence on the Egyptian soil, when hunger drove them from their native hills and valleys to the eastern provinces of the Pharaonic empire. Like the modern Bedouins, the Shasu were a pastoral people in the full sense of the word. The old name of the race of the Shasu and Shaus-Bedouins in the course of time became equivalent in the popular language to 'shepherds,' that is, a wandering people, who occupied themselves in bringing up cattle, which formed the only wealth

pronounced Shufu, was transcribed by Manetho Suphis. The older, and only correct pronunciation of this name has been carefully preserved in the Cheops of Herodotus.

of the inhabitants of the desert in all times down to the present day.

If the objection should be raised that the monuments (note well, those which have been discovered up to the present time) pass over in complete silence the name of Hyksos, this appearance of proof loses all its importance from the following consideration. By far the greater number of contemporary monuments which once existed as individual witnesses of the remembrance of the historical events under the rule of the foreign kings, have entirely disappeared from the surface of the Egyptian soil. It must be left to some lucky accident, that somewhere the stones now hidden or buried in the rubbish may come to the light of day, to give us new information about these portions of the history of the Egyptian empire, which are as obscure as they are important. The wonderland on the banks of the mighty Nile is a land of continual and startling discoveries, and will remain so for all coming times and generations. In the hope of finding important discoveries in the soil of Egypt in consequence of new excavations, we should esteem it unwise to give to our views the absolute form of a fixed unalterable judgment. But we may well be allowed to compare the information in the inscriptions of the few remains of the monuments which have been preserved with the accounts which the Greeks have handed down to us, and from this to form our own opinion, and leave it to the consideration of the future, if by a happy accident our conjectures should be confirmed or refuted.

At the present moment we expressly affirm the complete agreement of the name of Hyksos with the Egyptian double word we have mentioned above — Hak Shaus, that is, 'king of the Arabs,' or 'king of the shepherds,' — the probability of which is proved by the actual existence of a similar form in the term Hak Abisha, 'king (or prince) of the land of Abisha,' which we meet with in the hall of the tomb of Khnumhotep at Beni-Hassan. We will not, however, on the other hand, maintain that the appellation Hak Shans is the same which the bearers of it, of whatever descent they might boast, either formed of their own accord for themselves, or assumed on account of their office. It is far more probable that the Egyptians, when at last they drove away their tyrants of Semitic blood, gave these princes, who for several centuries had considered themselves as the legitimate kings of Egypt, the nickname Hak Shasu by way of a contemptuous expression.

An ancient tradition furnishes an important addition to the proofs of the Arab origin of the hated Hyksos kings, which has been preserved by several Arab historians of the Middle Ages. An Arab tradition tells us of a certain Sheddâd (the name means a powerful ruler), the son of Ad, who made an irruption into Egypt, conquered the country, and extended his victorious campaign as far as the Straits of Gibraltar. He and his descendants, the founders of the Amalekite dynasty, are said to have maintained themselves more than two hundred years in Lower Egypt, where they made the town 'Awaris their capital.*

According to another tradition, on the testimony of Africanus (one of those who extracted from the work of Manetho), the Hyksos kings were Phœnicians, who took possession of Memphis, and made the town of Auaris, or Awaris, in the Sethroite nome, their chief fortress. This tradition also is not without a certain air of truth, if the reader will recall to mind what I ventured to state above regarding the Char-Phœnicians and the town Auaris. The ancient seats of the Shasu-Arabs and of the Phœnicians extended towards the west as far as the same town of Zor-Tanis. The two races must therefore have been located together in the closest manner — the first as wanderers, the last as fixed inhabitants of the eastern provinces of the Egyptian empire, which were possessed by the foreigners.

* Compare Fluegel's *History of the Arabs*, 2d ed. p. 11.

That the cultivated Khar in such a mixture of nations claimed the first rank, can scarcely need proof. Whether they or the Shasu were the originators of this movement against the native kings of the empire, is a point for the decision of which scientific research has hitherto failed to discover the means.

Let us leave entirely the ground of conjectures and probabilities, and turn now to the monuments, to see if they can furnish us with any existing traces of these foreigners to assist our researches. The answer is decidedly in the affirmative, but in such a general way that further inspection and examination is very necessary. The inscriptions designate this foreign people, which once ruled in Egypt till it was driven from the country by the Theban kings, by the name of Men, or Menti. According to the great table of nations on the walls of the temple of Edfou, those called Menti are inhabitants of the land of Asher. By the help of the demotic translation of the inscription, in two languages, on the great stone of Tanis (known under the name of the decree of Canopus, a voucher, it is true, of the Ptolemaic times), we can establish that such was the common name of Syria in the mouths of the Egyptians who were then living; while the older name of the same country, in the hieroglyphic part of the stone, was Rutennu, with the addition, 'of the East.' In the different languages, and in the different times of history, the following names, Syria, Rutennu of the East, Asher, and Menti, were therefore synonymous. We wish here to point out, although we leave the matter undecided, that Asher, in late Egyptian, may perhaps have meant the Semitic Ashur, or Assyria, and at last may have become contracted both as to the extent of country and common usage to the well-known geographical term Syria.

Of high importance with regard to the foregoing question appears to us the derivation of the old national name Rutennu (or Lutennu), which, in the history of the eighteenth dynasty, and in the warlike campaigns of the pharaohs in the east, plays such an important part. As to the geographical extent to which this name applied, we are fortunately so well informed that no mistake can ever occur again. In the great catalogue of the towns of western Asia conquered by Thutmes III., whose inhabitants, after the battle of Megiddo, submitted to the Egyptian rule, they are described in a general superscription as all the population of 'the upper land of the Rutennu.' This proves, in the most positive manner, that the name of Upper Rutennu must have included in its circumference almost exactly the frontiers of the country which was later that of the twelve tribes of Israel.

With this key in our hand, we can open many a closed door to the right understanding of the great movement of nations to the east of Egypt, so that we can survey with a clear glance the horizon of these migrations. If it is an undeniable fact, resulting from historical inquiry under the guidance of the monuments, that, immediately after the driving out of the Menti, the Egyptian kings of the eighteenth dynasty planned their campaigns of conquest against the countries of western Asia inhabited by the Rutennu, then there lay at the bottom of these obstinate constantly repeated inroads a fixed feeling of revenge and retribution for losses and injuries received. The conviction forces itself upon us almost irresistibly, that the irruption of the foreigners into Egypt was made by the Syrians, who, in their campaigns through the arid deserts, found in the Shasu-Arabs welcome allies who well knew the country. And here I am reminded of a similar alliance which Cambyses formed with the Arabs in his campaign against Egypt. They found also in the Semitic inhabitants settled in the eastern provinces brothers of the same race, with whose assistance they succeeded in giving a death-blow to the Egyptian empire, and of

THE EXODUS OF ISRAEL. 105

robbing it for centuries of all power of action and independent life.

The present state of Egyptian inquiry, concerning the history of the Hyksos, has enabled us to find an answer to a number of questions which stand in close connection with these matters, and embrace the following facts: —

1. A certain number of non-Egyptian kings of foreign origin, belonging to the nation of the Menti, ruled for a long time in the eastern portion of the Delta.

2. The foreign princes had, besides the town Zoan, chosen as the capital of their power the typhonic place Hanar-Auaris, on the east side of the Pelusiac arm of the Nile, within what was called later the Sethroite nome, and had provided it with strong fortifications.

3. The foreigners had, besides the customs and manners, adopted the official language and the holy writing of the Egyptians. The whole arrangement of their court was formed on the Egyptian model.

4. These same foreign kings were patrons of art. Egyptian artists made, according to the old pattern and according to the prescribed usage of their forefathers, the monuments in honor of the foreign tyrants; yet, in the statues of them, they were obliged to give way with regard to the expression

of the foreign countenances, the peculiar arrangement of the beard, and the head-dress and other deviations of foreign costume.

5. These foreign kings honored, as the supreme god of their newly-acquired country, the son of the heavenly goddess Nut, the god Set or Sutekh, with the additional name Nub, 'gold,' or 'the golden,' — according to the Egyptian mode of viewing things, the origin of all that is bad and perverse in the seen and unseen world; the opponent of what is good, and the enemy of light. In the towns of Zoan and Auaris the foreigners had constructed to the honor of this god splendid temples and other monuments, especially sphinxes, constructed of stone from Syene.

6. In all probability one of the foreign lords was the originator of the new era, which most likely began with the first year of his reign. Up to the reign of the second Ramses, four hundred full years had elapsed of this reckoning, which was acknowledged by the Egyptians.

7. The Egyptians were indebted to the stay of the foreigners, and to their social intercourse with them, for much useful knowledge. Especially the horizon of their artistic views was enlarged, and new forms and shapes were introduced into Egyptian art, the Semitic origin of which is obvious from

a single glance at these productions. The winged Sphinx may be reckoned as a notable example of this new direction of art introduced from abroad.

We remarked above that the number of the monuments which contain memorials of the time of the Hyksos is very limited; and we must add that the names of the Hyksos kings, with which they ornamented their own memorial-stones (statues, sphinxes, and similar works), or those of earlier Egyptian kings of the times before them, have arrived to us half obliterated or carefully chiselled out, so that the decipherment of the faint traces which remain has to struggle with great difficulties. These important lacunæ in the study of the Egyptian monuments find a sufficient explanation in the proved and easily understood practice of the kings of native race who ascended the throne after the expulsion of the foreigners, and who particularly set themselves carefully to obliterate all remembrance of the hated princes, and to destroy and annihilate their works.

The names of the Hyksos kings, which are engraved on the more than life-size statue at Tell Mukhdam, the border of the stand of the colossal sphinxes in the Louvre, the lion found near Bagdad, the sacrificial stone in the Museum of Boulak, are scratched out with great care, so as to be almost undistinguishable; and science has to thank a happy accident for the preservation and decipherment of the names of two Hyksos kings. These are:

1. The king, whose first cartouche contains the name Ra aa-ab-taui, and whose second cartouche encloses the family name Apopi, or Apopa; and,

2. King Nubti, or Nub, with the official name Set aa-pe-huti (properly, 'Set the powerful').

The name of the first-mentioned king, which would be pronounced in the Memphitic dialect Aphophi, differs little from that of the Shepherd king Aphobis, or Aphophis, Apophis, which, according to the Manethonian tradition, was the fourth of the above-named Hyksos kings. We will also not withhold the remark, that many Egyptians of these times call themselves Apopi, or Apopa, in the same way, with a certain predilection.

The names which designate the other Hyksos kings are in a striking manner similar in sound with the names which the god 'Set-Nub the powerful' is accustomed to bear on the Egyptian monuments. Was it the intention of the foreign prince to be prayed to as the god Set?

In the deep obscurity in which a pitiless fate has hidden the history of the irruption and the dominion of the Hyksos kings in Egypt, a ray of light is visible only towards the close of the tyranny of the foreigners.

In a roll of papyrus in the British Museum (Sallier, No. 1) there is, although unfortunately much interrupted with lacunæ, the beginning of an historical description which is connected with the names of the foreign king Apopi and the Egyptian underking Ra-Sekenen (the victorious Sun-god Ra), both contemporaries. It is the glory of that master of science, E. de Rougé, too soon lost to us, to have first recognized the high value of this writing in its full importance. It begins with the following words: —

(I. 1) "It came to pass that the land of Kemi belonged to enemies. And nobody was lord in the day when that happened. At that time there was indeed a king Ra-Sekenen, but he was only a Hak of the town of the south, but the enemies sat in the town of the Amu, and there was king (Ur) (2) Apopi in the town of Auaris. And the whole world brought him its productions, also the northern land did the same with all the good things of Ta-meri; and the king Apopi (3) chose the god Set for his divine master, and he did not serve any of the gods which were worshipped in the whole land. He built him a temple of beautiful work, to last a long time [. . . and the king] (4) Apopi (appointed) feasts (and) days to offer (sacrifices) at each time to the god Sutech."

The king Ra-Sekenen in 'the city of the south' had, according to all appearance, incurred the particular displeasure of the tyrant of Auaris, who intended to hurl him from the throne, and sought for means and pretexts to carry out his intention.

There had evidently before this begun a correspondence between the tyrant in the north and the Hak in the southern land, in which the first-named among other things required of the last to give up the worship of his gods, and to worship Amon-Ra alone as the only divinity of the country. Ra-Sekenen had declared himself prepared for all, but had added a proviso to his letter, in which he expressly declared, to allow him to speak for himself (II. 1) "that he was not able to promise to serve any other of the gods which were worshipped in the whole country but Amon-Ra, the king of the gods alone."

A new message to the unfortunate Hak of the southern city was deliberated upon and agreed to by king Apopi. The papyrus announces this in these words: — " Many days later after these events (II. 2) King Apopi sent to the governor of the town in the land of the south this message, . . . which his secretaries had advised him. (3) And the messenger of Apopi betook himself to the governor of the city of the south. And (the messenger) was brought before the governor of the city of the south. (4) He spoke thus, when he spoke to the messenger of King Apopi: 'Who sent thee here to this city of the south? How hast thou come to spy out?'"

The messenger of king Apopi thus addressed, first answered the governor in these simple words, 'King Apopi it is who sends to thee;' and thereupon delivers his message, the particular contents of which are very disquieting to the first-mentioned personage. It was a question of stopping a canal. The first remark of the messenger that he had not taken sleep either day or night, until he had fulfilled his mission, must appear like scorn. The writer paints the situation of the Hak with few words, but those full of meaning.

" (6) And the governor of the town in the south was for a long time troubled so that he could not (7) answer the messenger of King Apopi."

But he nerved himself and made a speech to the messenger. Unfortunately the chief contents of it have been torn out by the destruction of the papyrus at this place. After the foreign messenger had been hospitably entertained, he betook himself back to the court of king Apopi, while Ra-Sekenen as quickly as possible called his friends around him. The papyrus thus relates what occurred:

"(11) And the messenger of King Apopi returned to the place where his lord tarried (III. 1). Thereupon the governor of the town of the south called unto him the great and chief men, as the commanders and captains who accompanied him, (2) in order (to communicate) to them the message which King Apopi had sent to him, but they all of one accord were silent through great grief, and wist not what to answer him good or bad.'"

After the following words, 'then sent King Apopi to the,' the writer breaks off in the middle of a sentence, without satisfying the curiosity of his readers two-and-thirty centuries afterwards. For next comes the beginning of the letters of Pentaur, the poet of the well-known heroic song of the great deeds of Ramses II. at Kadesh.

Although this precious writing is frequently, in the most important passages of the narrative of Apopi, interrupted through holes and rents, owing to the splitting of the papyrus, still what remains is amply sufficient to make known to us the persons, the places, and the circumstances of this historical drama.

King Apopi meets us as chief hero. His royal residence is in Auaris. The enemies, foreigners, have taken possession of Egypt. Its inhabitants are obliged to pay a tax of their possessions and substance to the foreign tyrants. Apopi worships his own divinity, the god Sutech, who is already known to us as the Egyptian expression of the Semitic Baal, especially of Baal Zapuna, the Baal-zephon of Holy Scripture. He builds a splendid temple to his god, and appoints festivals and offerings for him.

In the south of the land, in No, 'the town' of the south, that is in Thebes, the capital of Patoris, 'the region of the south' (the biblical Pathros), there sat an offshoot of the oppressed pharaohs, Ra-Sekenen, only invested with the title of Hak, or sub-king.

King Apopi is the all-powerful lord, the general ruler of the land. Complaisant learned men belong to his court, who bear the remarkable title of Rechichet, that is, the experts.* They give counsel to the king, bad counsel as it appears, since they induce him to send a messenger to the sub-king in No, with still more severe demands worthy of a Cambyses. The messenger enjoys no rest, but day and night hurries to the southern land.

The sub-king, Ra-Sekenen, receives him with the

* On the stone of Tanis the Greek translator renders this term by the well-known word *Hierogrammats*, or Temple scribes.

same question which Joseph, his contemporary, put to his own brethren when they came down to Egypt to buy corn, since he said to them, 'Whence come ye? Ye are spies, and ye are come here to see where the land is open.'

After the Hak had received all the communications of the tyrant Apopi from the mouth of his messenger, he was deeply moved by their dangerous import. The great lords and chief men of his court were summoned to a council; and the leaders also of the army, the Uau or officers, and the Hauti or captains, took part in it.

But good counsel is dear. No one dared to make any proposal from the fear of unfortunate consequences.

Such is an abstract of this remarkable document. We may rest assured, even without knowing the conclusion of the whole story, that the author of it must have aimed, by his description, at portraying something more important than the humiliation of a native Hak. The subject without doubt really was the history of the uprising of the Egyptians against the yoke of the foreigners. In order to teach us the cause and meaning of this, the unknown narrator begins his history of the war of liberation, which was brought about in the way we have mentioned, by a description of the unfortunate position of the

THE EXODUS OF ISRAEL. 115

empire. His history, which began so sadly, ends happily, and the actual proofs from the monuments bear out his fortunate conclusion.

In order to find the proofs from the monuments, let us betake ourselves to the land of the south, let us pass by the towns of Thebes, Hermonthis, and Latopolis, on both sides of the stream, and let us stop on the right bank, in sight of the most ancient walls of the city of El-Kab. This discovers to us the position and extent of the former capital of the third upper Egyptian nome, which the Greeks designated as the town of Eileithyia, the 'goddess presiding over births,' and the Romans as the town of Lúcina in their description of Egyptian places. In the background towards the east there rise rocky hills, with long rows of tombs, whose dark openings appear to the traveller like the broken windows of a ruined castle.

We will betake ourselves to the chambers of the tombs.

In truly venerable forms, which seem to people the chambers of the dead, we greet the contemporaries of the Hyksos kings, whose progeny belonged to the heroes of the great war of liberation of the Egyptians from the tyranny of the foreigners.

Let us enter these chambers of the dead, which a grandson has dedicated to the hero Aahmes, the son of Abana-Baba, and his whole house as the last memorial of their existence and of their deeds. The walls of the narrow chamber are covered by a widely-spread genealogical tree of his race, which has suffered much injury.

Aahmes, the son of Baba-Abana, and his daughter's son Fahir, form the most important persons of the genealogical tree.

We will lay before the reader a faithful translation of the inscription in which Aahmes portrayed in the old speech the course of his life as a picture of the time for posterity. The actual author of the inscription is 'the son of his daughter, who executed the work in this sepulchral chamber, in order to perpetuate the name of the father of his mother, the master of the drawing art of Amon, Pahir.'

The following are the words of the inscription as the clever Pahir executed it:

1. The deceased chief of the sailors, Aahmes, a son of Abana
2. speaks thus. I speak to you, to all people, and I give you to know the honorable praise which was given to me. I was presented with a golden chain eight times in the sight
3. of the whole land, and with male and female slaves in great numbers. I had a possession of many acres. The surname of 'the brave' which I gained never vanished away

4. in this land. He speaks also further. I have completed my youthful wandering in the town of Nukheb. My father was a captain of the deceased Ra Sekenen, Baba

5. son of Roant, was his name. Then I became captain in his place on the ship 'The Calf,' in the time of the lord of the country, Aahmes, the deceased.

6. I was still young and unmarried, and was girded with the garment of the band of youths. Still, after I had prepared for myself a house, I was taken

7. on the ship 'The North,' because of my strength. It was my duty to accompany the great lord — life, prosperity, and health attend him! — on foot, when he rode in his chariot.

8. They besieged the town of Auaris. My duty was to be valiantly on foot before his holiness. Then was I changed

9. to the ship 'Ascent in Memphis.' They fought by sea on the lake Pazetku of Auaris. I fought in a struggle with fists, and

10. I gained a hand. This was shown to the herald of the king. They gave me a golden present for my bravery. After that a new fight arose in this place, and anew I fought in a struggle with fists

11. in that place, and I gained a hand. They gave me a golden present another time. And they fought at the place Takem to the south of the town (Auaris).

12. I gained of living prisoners a grown-up man. I went into the water — him also bringing to remain aside from the road to

13. the town. I went, firmly holding him, through the water. They announced me to the herald of the king. Then I was presented with a golden present again. They

14. conquered Auaris. I gained in that place prisoners, a grown-up man and three women, which makes in all three heads. His holiness gave them to me for my possession as slaves.

15. They besieged the town Sherohan in the sixth year. His holiness took it. I brought booty home from here, two women and a hand.

16. They gave me a golden present for valor. In addition, the prisoners from it were given to me as slaves. After then that his holiness had mown down the Syrians of the land of Asia,

17. he went against Khont-Hon-nofer to smite the mountaineers of Nubia. His holiness made a great destruction among them.

18. I carried booty away from that place, two living grown-up men and three hands. I was presented with a golden gift another time; they also gave me three female slaves.

19. His holiness descended the stream. His heart was joyful because of brave and victorious deeds. He had taken possession of the south and of the north land. There came an enemy from the southern region.

20. He approached. His advantage was the number of his people. The gods of the southern land were against his fist. His holiness found him at the water Tent-ta-tot. His holiness brought him forth

21. as a living prisoner. All his people brought booty back. I brought back two young men, when I had cut them off from the ship of the enemy. They

22. gave me five heads, besides my share of five hides of arable land in my town. It happened thus to all the ship's crew in the same way. Twice

23. there came that enemy whose name was Teta. He

had assembled with him a bad set of fellows. His holiness annihilated him and his men, so that they no longer existed. So there were

24. given to me three people and five hides of arable land in my town. I conveyed by water the deceased king Amenhotep I., when he went up against Kush to extend

25. the borders of Egypt. He smote these Nubians by means of his warriors. Being pressed closely, they could not escape. Bewildered

26. they remained in the place just as if they were nothing. Then I stood at the head of our warriors, and I fought as was right. His holiness admired my valor. I gained two hands,

27. and brought them to his holiness. They sought after their inhabitants and their herds. I brought down a living prisoner and brought him to his holiness. I brought his holiness in two days to Egypt

28. from Khnumt-hirt (that is, the upper spring). Then I was presented with a golden gift. Then I brought forward two female slaves, besides those which I led

29. to his holiness, and I was raised to the dignity of a 'champion of the prince.' I conveyed the deceased King Thutmes I., when he ascended by water to Chonthon-nofer,

30. to put an end to the strife among the inhabitants, and to stop the attacks on the land side. And I was brave (before him) on the water. It went badly on the (attack)

31. of the ship on account of its upsetting. They raised me to the rank of a captain of the sailors. His holiness — may life, prosperity, and health be allotted to him! —

32. (Here follows a rent, which, according to the context, is to be filled up in such a manner as to show that a new occasion calls the king to war against the people of the south.)

33. His holiness raged against them like a panther, and his holiness slung his first dart, which remained sticking in the body of his enemy. He

34. fell fainting down before the royal diadem. There was then in a short time a (great defeat), and their people were taken away as living enemies.

35. And his holiness travelled downwards. All nations were in his power. And this wretched king of the Nubian people found himself bound on the fore part of the ship of his holiness, and he was placed on the ground

36. in the town of Thebes. After this his holiness betook himself to the land of the Rutennu, to cool his anger among the inhabitants of the land. His holiness reached the land of Naharina.

37. His holiness found — life, prosperity, and health to him! — these enemies. He ordered the battle. His holiness made a great slaughter among them.

38. The crowd of the living prisoners was innumerable, which his majesty carried away in consequence of his victory. And behold, I was at the head of our warriors. His holiness admired my valor.

39. I carried off a chariot of war and its horses, and those which were upon it, as living prisoners, and brought them to his holiness. Then I was afterwards presented with gold.

40. Now I have passed many days and reached a gray old age. My lot will be that of all men upon the earth. [I shall go down into the lower world, and be placed in the] coffin, which I have made for myself.

The hard time of distress and tyranny was now past for the Egyptian people. The reign of oppression was at once broken up, when Auaris had fallen, and another town of the Hyksos, the fortress Sherohan, had been taken by storm. In the sixth year of the reign of king Aahmes, the founder of the eighteenth house of the pharaohs, Kemi was at length freed from the long oppression of the foreigner, and the armed soldiers of the pharaoh passed triumphantly through the lands of the south and the east of Egypt, to conquer what had been lost, and 'to wash their heart,' that is, to cool their anger against the enemies from a foreign land. Yet we must not forestall the events, the true portraying of which the simple narratives of two warriors of those days have handed down to us, and we will next cast another glance at the conclusion of the seventeenth dynasty.

King Taä III., with the surname of 'the brave,' the predecessor of the Pharaoh Aahmes, the conqueror of Auaris, reigned in No-Thebes. His attention was directed to the creation of a Nile flotilla, with the intention one day of conquering Auaris, which was under the dominion of the Lower Egyptian Netherlands.

His successor, of the name of Kames, seems only to have reigned a short time. He was the husband of the much venerated queen Aah-hotep, whose coffin with the golden ornaments on the body was some years ago found by some Theban agriculturists in the ancient necropolis of No, buried only a few feet below the surface of the soil.* These venerable artistic and historically precious remains of Egyptian antiquity, were delivered over to the Museum of Boolaq.

* The cover of the coffin has the shape of a mummy, and it is gilt above and below. The holy royal asp decks the brow. The eyelids are gilt. The white of the eyes is represented by quartz, and the pupils by black glass. A rich imitation necklace covers the breast and shoulders; the Uræus serpent and the vulture — the holy symbols of the Upper and the Lower land of Kemi — lie below the necklace. A closed pair of wings seems to protect the rest of the body. At the soles of the feet stand the statues of the mourning goddesses Isis and Nephthys. The inscription in the middle row gives us the name of the queen, Aah-hotep, that is, 'servant of the moon.'

When the coffin was opened, there were found between the linen coverings precious weapons and ornaments: daggers, a golden axe, a chain with three large golden bees, and a breastplate. On the body itself was found a golden chain with a scarabæus attached, armlets, a fillet for the brow, and other objects. Two little ships in gold and silver, bronze axes, and great bangles for the ankles, lay immediately upon the wood of the coffin.

The richest and the most precious of the ornaments showed the shields of the Pharaoh Aahmes. He bears on them the surname of Nakht, that is, 'the brave or victorious.' Without doubt, then, Queen Aah-hotep was buried in Thebes during the reign of her son Aahmes. Mention has already been made of the tomb of her royal husband at Thebes. Aah-hotep is therefore the proper ancestress of the eighteenth dynasty. It was her son Aahmes who was destined to rise up as the avenger of his native country for the shame and oppression which it had so long endured. If therefore Apopi was the pharaoh that honored Joseph, Aahmes was the king that succeeded him.

And yet a strange enigma covers this age of shame, the veil of which we are not yet able to lift. For on a minute examination of the monuments of the times of the seventeenth and eighteenth dynasties, many well-founded reflections force themselves upon us involuntarily; since, in fact, it would seem as if the hatred of the Egyptians against the Hyksos kings had not been so intense as the story handed down by Manetho appears to represent it. We of course except, when we speak of the Egyptians, the legitimate but oppressed kings of 'the region of the south,' in the Upper country, to whom the foreign tyrants in the Lowlands must have appeared in no agreeable light.

Between the Egyptian and Semitic races — and whatever may have been the exact complexion and descent of the latter — there certainly was no deep-rooted hereditary enmity, as the interpreters would make us believe. There was, indeed, a hatred on the part of the Theban race of kings, to whom their humiliation by the foreigners appeared all the more unendurable, as they had not the strength and power to free themselves from their dependence on the foreign lords of the Netherlands. They had only at their command the weapon of the weaker against the stronger — namely, an exaggeration of the real existing relations between them — by picturing the foreigners as relentless against everything native. Hence they derived consolation, and an excuse for their own incapability to shake off the yoke, and to regain the firm possession of the whole kingdom.

We will simply put the question, If those foreign kings were in fact desecrators of the temples, devastators and destroyers of the works of bygone ages, how is it that these ancient works, although only the last remains of them, still exist, and especially in the chief seats of the Hyksos dominion; and further, that these foreign kings allowed their names to be engraved as memorial witnesses on the works of the native pharaohs? Instead of destroying they preserved them, and sought by appropriate measures to perpetuate themselves and their remembrance on the monuments already existing of former rulers.

Zoan-Tanis, the capital of the Egyptian eastern provinces, with its world of temples and statues of the times of the sixth, twelfth, and thirteenth dynasties, had so little to suffer from the Hyksos, that on the contrary these princes thought it incumbent upon them to increase the splendor of this vast temple-town by their own constructions, although in a Semitic style of execution.

To the Theban kings of the eighteenth dynasty must first be attributed the doubtful praise of mak-

THE EXODUS OF ISRAEL. 125

ing war on the dead stones as a vengeance against the Hyksos kings, which their forefathers had in vain sought to wreak on the living monarchs. To destroy the monuments of the opposition kings, to annihilate their names and titles so as to render them unrecognizable, and to falsify historical truth by inscribing their own names, such was the system invented by the Egyptian pharaohs, who set about their work with such success as nearly to root out from the face of the earth the contemporary memorials of the Hyksos kings. We have to thank this persecution for the difficulties which lie in the way of restoring the history of the most ancient domination of the foreigners in Egypt.

Before we conclude this chapter, perhaps we may be allowed to make some remarks on the relation, in point of time, of these historical events, with the stay of the Hyksos on one side, and on the other side with the stay of the children of Israel, on Egyptian soil. We have already made mention of a memorial stone of the time of the second Ramses found in Tanis, the inscription on which commences with the following indication of its date: 'In the year 400, on the 4th day of the month Mesori of King Nub.' As on the basis of the newest and best inquiries into the question of old Egyptian chronology we fix the reign of Ramses II. at the year 1350 B. C. as a mean rate between various proposals, the reign of the Hyksos king Nub, and probably the beginning of his reign, would fall about the year 1750 B. C., that is, four hundred years before Ramses II. Although we are completely in the dark as to what place king Nub occupied in the succession of the princes of his house, yet the number mentioned has a certain importance in fixing an approximative date for the stay of the foreign kings in Egypt. This importance becomes much enhanced by its very clear relation to a similar statement in Holy Writ in relation to the total duration of the stay of the children of Israel in Egypt. According to this statement (Exodus xii. 40) the Hebrews from the time of the immigration of their ancestor Jacob till the exodus had remained four hundred and thirty years in Egypt. In another place (Genesis xv. 13) the duration of their stay is expressed by the round number of four hundred years. Now, as according to general acceptation the exodus from Egypt took place after the death of Ramses II., the pharaoh of the oppression, the year 1300 will approximately correspond to the time of the exodus in the reign of Mineptah, the son and successor of Ramses II. If we add, therefore, four hundred and thirty years as the expression for the total duration of the stay of the Hebrews in Egypt, we arrive at

THE EXODUS OF ISRAEL. 127

the year 1730 B. C. as the approximative date of the immigration of Jacob into Egypt, and for the time of the official career of his son Joseph at the court of pharaoh. In other words, we arrive at the conclusion that the time of Joseph (1730 B. C.) must have fallen in the time of the Hyksos' domination, about the reign of the previously mentioned foreign prince, Nub (1750).

This singular coincidence of numbers, as we openly admit, appears to us to have a higher value than the data fixed on the grounds of particular calculations of the chronological tables of Manetho and the fathers of the church. For these numbers neither change nor rectify the great building of general chronology. Their importance is of quite a different character. Independently of every kind of arrangement and combination of numbers, they prove the probability of a fixed date for a very important section of the general history of the world on the grounds of two chronological data, which in a most striking way correspond with one another, and of which each separately has its origin in an equally trustworthy and respectable source.

The supposition that Joseph was sold into Egypt and afterwards rose to great honor under the Hyksos, as results from the chronological relations we have mentioned, receives fresh support for its probability from a Christian tradition preserved by V. Syncellus. According to this tradition 'received by the whole world,' Joseph ruled the land in the reign of king Aphophis (Apopi of the monuments), whose age within a few years corresponds with the commencement of the eighteenth dynasty.

We have great satisfaction in adding another very remarkable and clear confirmation of our remarks upon the time of Joseph and his master the pharaoh. Upon the grounds of an old Egyptian inscription hitherto unknown, whose author must have been a contemporary of Joseph and his family, we hope to adduce a proof that Joseph and the Hyksos cannot henceforth be separated from one another.

As a previous remark we will recall to the recollection of our readers the well-known fact that in the days of the patriarch in Egypt a seven years' famine occurred, the consequence of a deficiency of water in the overflowing of the Nile at that time.

This inscription, which appears to us so important, exists in one of the tombs at El-Kab, of which we have before spoken more particularly. From the peculiarities of the language, and from the style of the internal pictorial decoration of the rock chambers, but principally from the name of its former possessor, Baba, we may consider that the tomb was erected in the times immediately preceding the eighteenth dynasty. Although no royal cartouche ornaments the walls of the tomb to give us certain information about the exact time of its erection, yet the following considerations are calculated to inform us on this point, and fortunately to fill up the gaps.

The name of the old possessor of the tomb, Baba, is already well known to us. Among the members of the great family of the times of the thirteenth dynasty, whose genealogical tree we have before laid before our readers, and the greater number of whose tombs are situated in the rocky city of the dead at El-Kab, Baba appears in the third generation as the additional name of a certain Sebek-tut, the father of queen Nubkhas. In the genealogical tree of the family of the Captain Aahmes at El-Kab the name Baba appears on another occasion, and also as the second appellation of our hero, Abana, a captain under king Ra-Sekenen (Taa III.). Unless we are mistaken, it is this Baba whose tomb, situated near that of Aahmes at El-Kab, promises us important disclosures. For the whole descendants of Aahmes, children, and grandchildren, and great-grandchildren, repose in their ancestors' tomb, and in the excavations of the rock which Pabir, once the governor of Eileithyia, had prepared for himself and them. We should, however, in vain look round the sepulchral chambers of the ancestors of Baba, were it not for the rock tomb of a Baba in the neighborhood of that we have already mentioned. The inscription, which exists in the hall of sacrifice of this tomb on the wall opposite to the door of entrance, contains the following simple childlike representation of his happy existence on earth, owing to his great riches in point of children:

"The chief at the table of princes, Baba, the risen again, he speaks thus: I loved my father, I honored my mother; my brother and my sisters loved me. I stepped out of the door of my house with a benevolent heart; I stood there with refreshing hand, and splendid were the preparations of what I collected for the feast-day. Mild was (my) heart, free from noisy anger. The gods bestowed upon me a rich fortune on earth. The city wished me health and a life full of freshness. I punished the evil-doers. The children which stood opposite to me in the town during the days which I have fulfilled were small as well as great, 60; there were prepared for them as many beds, chairs (?) as many, tables (?) as many. They all consumed 120 Epha of Durra, the milk of 3 cows, 52 goats, and 9 she-asses, of balsam a hin, and of oil 2 jars.

"My speech may appear a joke to some opponent. But I call as witness the god Month that my speech

THE EXODUS OF ISRAEL. 131

is true. I had all this prepared in my house; in addition I gave cream in the pantry and beer in the cellar in a more than sufficient number of hin measures.

"I collected the harvest, a friend of the harvest god. I was watchful at the time of sowing. And now when a famine arose, lasting many years, I issued out corn to the city at each famine." *

There ought not to be the smallest doubt as to whether the last words of the inscription relate to an historical fact or not; to something definite or something only general. Strongly as we are inclined to recognize a general way of speaking in the narrative of Ameni, where 'years of famine' are spoken of, here we are compelled by the context of the report before us to understand the term 'the many years' of the famine which arose as relating to a definite historical time. For famines following one another on account of a deficiency of water in the overflowing of the Nile were of the greatest rarity, and history knows and mentions only one example of it, namely, the seven years' famine of the pharaoh of Joseph. Besides, Baba (or if the term is preferred, the Babas, for the most part the contemporaries of the thirteenth and seventeenth dynasties), about the same time as Joseph exercised

* Or also, 'to each hungry person.'

his office under one of the Hyksos kings, lived and worked under the native king Ra-Sekenen (Taa III.) in the old town of El-Kab. The only just conclusion is that the many years of famine in the time of Baba must precisely correspond with the seven years of famine under Joseph's pharaoh, one of the shepherd kings.

We leave it to the judgment of the reader to arrive at a conclusion on the probability of a clear connection between the two different reports on the same extraordinary occurrence. The simple words of the biblical account and the inscription in the tomb of Baba are too clear and convincing, to leave any room for reproach on the ground of possible error. The account in Holy Scripture of the elevation of Joseph under one of the Hyksos kings, of his life at their court, of the reception of his father and brothers in Egypt with all their belongings, is in complete accordance with the manners and customs, as also with the place and time.

Joseph's Hyksos-Pharaoh reigned in Auaris, or Zoan, the later Ramses-town, and held his court in the Egyptian style, but without excluding the Semitic language. His pharaoh has proclaimed before him in Semitic language an Abrek, that is, 'bow the knee,' a word which is still retained in the hieroglyphic dictionary, and was adopted by the Egyptians to express their feeling of reverence at the sight of an important person or object. He bestows on him the high dignity of a Zaphnatpaneakh, 'governor of the Sethroitic nome.* On the Egyptian origin of the offices of an Adon and Ab which Joseph attributes to himself before his family, I have already made all the remarks that are necessary. The name of his wife Asnat is pure Egyptian and almost entirely confined to the old and middle empire. It is derived from the very common female name Sant, or Snat. The father of his wife, the priest of On-Heliopolis, is a pure Egyptian, whose name Potiphera meant in the native language Putiper'a (or pher'a), 'the gift of the sun.' The chamberlain who bought the boy Joseph from his brothers, and whose wife tempted the virtue of the young servant, was Putipher, a name which could not be pronounced in Egyptian otherwise than Putipar or (phar), 'the gift of the risen one.' His titles are given in Semitic language, although the word Saris, or chamberlain, is found written with Egyptian letters.

* Pa'anekh, ' the place of life,' was the peculiar designation of the capital of this nome in the holy writing. The whole long word is to be analyzed into its component parts in the old Egyptian language.

Za   p-   u   nt   p-   a   'anekh.
' Governor of the district of the place of life.'

We will not neglect at the mention of Putiphar's wife to call attention to the passage of the Orbiney papyrus, which at the same time is calculated to cast a bad light on the wantonness of the Egyptian women, but which before all things stands in a particular relation to the history of Joseph. Anepu, a married man, sends his young brother, the unmarried hero of the story, from the field to the house to fetch seed corn. What occurred the following literal translation sufficiently explains:—"And he sent his little brother, and said to him, 'Hasten and bring us seed corn from the village.' And his little brother found the wife of his elder brother occupied in combing her hair. And he said to her 'Rise up, give me seed corn that I may return to the field, for thus has my elder brother enjoined me, to return without delaying.' The woman said to him, 'Go in, open the chest, that thou mayst take what thine heart desires, for otherwise my locks will fall to the ground.' And the youth went within into the stable, and took thereout a large vessel, for it was his will to carry out much seed corn. And he loaded himself with wheat and Durra corn, and went out with it. Then she said to him, 'How great is the burden in thine arms?' He said to her, 'Two measures of Durra and three measures of wheat make together five measures which rest on my

-arms.' Thus he spake to her. But she spake to the youth and said, 'How great is thy strength! Well have I remarked thy power many a time.' And her heart knew him! ... and she stood up and laid hold of him, and she said to him, 'Come, let us celebrate an hour's repose. The most beautiful things shall be thy portion, for I will prepare for thee festal garments.' Then was the youth like to the panther of the south for rage, on account of the evil word which she had spoken to him. But she was afraid beyond all measure. And he spoke to her and said, 'Thou, O woman, hast been like a mother to me, and thy husband like a father, for he is older than I, so that he might have been my begetter. Why this great sin that thou hast spoken to me? Say it not to me another time, then will I this time not tell it, and no word of it shall come out of my mouth to any man at all.' And he loaded himself with his burden and went out into the field. And he went to his elder brother; and they completed their day's work. And when it was evening the elder brother returned home to his habitation. And his little brother followed behind his oxen, which he had laden with all the good things of the field, to prepare for them their place in the stable in the village. And behold the wife of his elder brother feared because of the word which she had spoken, and she took a jar of fat, and she was like one to whom an evil-doer had offered violence, since she wished to say to her husband, 'Thy little brother has offered me violence.' And her husband returned home at evening, according to his daily custom, and found his wife lying stretched out and suffering from injury. She gave him no water for his hands according to her custom. And the candles were not lighted, so that the house was in darkness. But she lay there. And her husband spoke to her thus, 'Who has had to do with thee? Lift thyself up!' She said to him, 'No one has had to do with me except thy little brother, since when he came to take seed corn for thee, he found me sitting alone, and said to me, "Come, let us make merry an hour and repose! Let down thy hair!" Thus he spake to me, but I did not listen to him (but said), See! am I not thy mother, and is not thy elder brother like a father to thee? Thus spoke I to him, but he did not hearken to my speech, and used force with me, that I might not tell thee. Now if thou allowest him to live, I will kill myself.'"

We will break off at this place the thread of the narrative in which the simple mode of speech and exposition corresponds in the most striking manner with the style of the Bible. What we want to point out, the reader of the foregoing sentences will immediately perceive. Potiphar's wife and Anepu's wife precisely resemble one another, and Joseph's and Bata's resistance and virtue appear so closely allied that one is almost inclined to assign a common origin to both traditions. In any case the passage we have just quoted from the Egyptian poem of the two brothers is a most precious and important elucidation of the history of Joseph in Egypt.

That Joseph was in fact clothed with the highest rank at court next to his king is evident from the office he filled of an Adon 'over all Egypt;' (compare Genesis xlv. 9.) On the monuments Adon answers to the Greek Epistates, an overseer, one set over others. The rank varied according to the business each had to perform. We find an Adon of the Amon town Diospolis, of the seat of justice, of the infantry, of the royal harem, of the treasury, of the workshops of pharaoh, of the beer-cellars, &c. The office of Joseph was quite different as an 'Adon over the whole land,' which I have only once again found in an old Egyptian inscription. Before king Horemheb of the eighteenth dynasty (the Horus of Manetho) ascended the throne, according to the account of a monument preserved at Turin, he was clothed with several very high offices, which brought him near to the person of the king. Finally the pharaoh was so pleased with his good services that he named him Ro-hir, that is Epitropos, or Proeurator of the whole land. In this capacity, without having any one to share his authority with him, he was called to be 'the great lord in the king's house,' and 'he gave answer to the king and pleased him with the utterances of his mouth.' In such a service was Horemheb 'an Adon of the whole land for the duration of many years,' until he rose to the position of 'heir of the throne of the whole land,' and finally placed the royal crown on his head. We see from this that an 'Adon of the whole land' was so important a position that Joseph, in fact, deserved the appellation of a Moshel, or Shallith, that is, a Prince or Regent over the whole land, as Luther translated the Hebrew word. With these remarks on Joseph, we will conclude this portion of the history of the middle empire.

CHAPTER VIII.

THE EIGHTEENTH DYNASTY. — THUTMES III.

KEEPING in view our main purpose, of dwelling chiefly upon such portions of Egyptian history as concern more nearly the biblical narrative, a large space has been given to the Hyksos and to the relations with Semitic tribes. We have now come to the eighteenth dynasty, which succeeded the foreign domination. Aahmes, the conqueror, was the first, and after him came several illustrious kings, each one bearing the name of Thutmes or Amenhotep. In many respects this is the most interesting period in the long annals. Thutmes III., perhaps the greatest of all the pharaohs, reigned fifty-three years, and was justly renowned throughout all the known world. He is the Alexander the Great of Egyptian history. He carried on no less than thirteen campaigns in foreign countries, and made the power of Egypt felt in the heart of Africa, as well as of Asia. Countless memorials of his reign exist in papyri, on temple walls, in tombs, and even upon scarabæi and other ornaments.

In still clear characters may be read most of the accounts of these wars, the numbers of troops that were engaged, the numbers killed and taken prisoners, and all the details of the vast booty brought into Egypt. When so many periods are in utter darkness, it is wonderful that such full records exist of this great reign. The statistician can easily form an idea of the civilization of the age by observing the quantity and character of the spoil and of the tributes afterwards imposed upon the conquered nations. Both the quantity and the character of the merchandise fill the mind of the modern reader with wonder. Meanwhile the monarch constructed new temples at Thebes and enlarged the old ones, and everywhere his triumphs were blazoned. The Roman emperor Germanicus, as Tacitus has recorded, saw these temples and their inscriptions when their glory had not been so far obscured.

Among the records of that day were catalogues of the towns and cities in Syria that had submitted to the Egyptian arms. One of these catalogues is filled with Semitic names.

What gives the highest value to the catalogue is the undisputed fact that more than three hundred years before the entrance of the Jews into the land of Canaan, a great league of peoples of the same race, which the monuments call by the name of the

Ruthen, existed in Palestine under little kings, who dwelt in the same towns and fortresses as we find stated on the monuments, and who for the greater part by conquest fell into the hands of the Jewish immigrants. Among these the king of Kadesh, on the Orontes, in the land of the Amorites — as the inscriptions expressly state — played the first part, since there obeyed him, as their chief leader, all the kings and their peoples from the water of Egypt (which is the same as the biblical brook, which flowed as the boundary of Egypt) to the rivers of Naharain, afterwards called Mesopotamia. To these had joined themselves the Phœnician Khalu, who dwelt in the country on the sea-coast called Zahi by the Egyptians, and whose capital was Aradus, as also the Kiti (the Chittim of Holy Scripture), who possessed the island of Cyprus, and in all probability the sea-coast lying to the north of the Phœnicians. The triangle between the points Kadesh, Semyra, and Aradus, represented the theatre of the hostile engagements which have been so often mentioned.

An unknown poet, out of the number of the holy fathers, felt himself inspired to sing in measured words the glory of the king, and the might and grandeur of the god Amon. His song has outlived the ravages of time and the enmity of man.

Having been well concealed, the tall granite tablet adorns at this day the rooms of the Egyptian Museum at Boolaq. As Moses, after the overthrow of pharaoh and his host in the Reedy Sea, sang a fervent hymn of praise to exalt the wondrous might and strength of the eternal God, so, three hundred years before the wise legislator of the Jewish people, the nameless seer of Amon praised, after his own fashion, his god and his king. Thus run his words: —

1. "Come to me," said Amon, " and enjoy yourself, and admire my excellences.
   Thou, my son, who honorest me, Thutmes the 3d, ever living.
   I shine in the light of the morning sun through thy love.
2. And my heart is enraptured, if thou directest thy noble step to my Temple.
   I stand upright there
3. In my dwelling.
   Therefore will I mark thee out as wonderful. I give thee power and victory over all lands.
   All people shall feel a terror before thy soul,
   And shall fear thee to the utmost ends of the world, to the
4. four props of Heaven.
   I let thy strength grow great in all bodies.
   I let thy war-cry resound in all the lands of foreign peoples.
   Let the kings of the world be all at once in thy grasp.

THE EXODUS OF ISRAEL. 143

5. I stretch out my own hands.
   I bind thee with bands, and enclose for thee the wandering Nubians to ten thousands and thousands.
   Those who inhabit the north, let them be taken prisoners by hundreds of thousands.
6. I place thy gainsayers under thy feet.
   Strike the host of thine enemies.
   Also I give thee the earth, in its length and in its breadth.
   Let the inhabitants of the west and of the east be thy subjects.
7. Pass through with joyful heart the lands which none have trodden till thy time.
   I will be thy leader; reach them;
   pass through the great ring of water
8. In the land of Naharain, in full victorious power.
   It is my will that the peoples hear thy war-cry, which penetrates to their caverns.
   I have taken away from their nostrils the breath of life.
9. I make thy manly courage penetrate even to their hearts.
   My crown on thy head is a consuming fire;
   It goes forth and conquers the false brood of the Kittim.
10. By the sparkle of its flames thé lords among them are turned to ashes.
    It cuts off the heads of the 'Aamu; they cannot escape;
    It strikes to the ground whoever turns himself round before its strength.
11. I make thy victories to go on through all nations;

My royal serpent shines on thy forehead,
And thy enemy is reduced to nothing as far as the horizon.
They come and bring the tribute on their shoulders,
And bow themselves
12. Before thy Holiness; for such is my will.
I make the rebellious ones fall down exhausted near thee,
A burning fire in their hearts, and in their limbs a trembling.
13. I came, and thou smotest the princes of Zahi.
I scatter them under thy feet over all their lands.
I make them behold thy Holiness like the beaming (sun).
Thou shinest in sight of them in my form.
14. I came, and thou smotest those who dwell in Asia.
Thou madest prisoners the goatherds of Ruthen.
I make them behold thy Holiness in the adornment of thy royal dignity,
As thou graspest the weapons on the war-chariots.
15. I came, and thou smotest the land of the East,
Thou camest to those who dwell in the territories of the Holy Land.
I make them behold thy Holiness like the star Canopus,
Which pours his light in a glance of fire
When he disperses the morning dew.
16. I came, and thou smotest the land of the West,
Kefa (Phœnicia) and Asebi (Cyprus) fear thee.
I make them behold thy Holiness like a young bull.
Full of courage, when he whets his horns, he is unapproachable.
17. I came, and thou smotest the subjects of their lords;

THE EXODUS OF ISRAEL.

The land of Mathen trembles for fear of thee.
I make them behold thy Holiness like a crocodile,
The terrible one in the water; he is not to be encountered.

18. I came, and thou smotest the islanders in the middle of the great sea;
Thy war-cry is over them.
I make them behold thy Holiness as the avenger,
Who appears on the back of his sacrifice.

19. I came, and thou smotest the land of the Thuhen;
The people of Uthent is in thy power.
I make them behold thy Holiness as a lion, with a fierce eye,
Who leaves his den and stalks through the valleys.

20. I came, and thou smotest the hinder lands,
The circuit of the Great Sea is bound in thy grasp.
I make them behold thy Holiness like the hovering sparrow-hawk.
Which seizes with his glance whatever pleases him.

21. I came, and thou smotest the lands in front;
Those who sit upon the sand thou hast made prisoners alive.
I make them behold thy Holiness like the jackal of the south;
A concealed wanderer he passes through the land.

22. I came, and thou smotest the nomad tribes of Nubia,
Even to the land of Shat, which is in thy grasp.
I make them behold thy Holiness like thy pair of brothers,
Whose hands I have united to bless thee.

23. As for thy pair of sisters, I make them shed on thee good fortune and prosperity.
My hands in the height of heaven ward off misfortune;

I protect thee, my beloved son,
The powerful bull, who didst stand up as king in Thebes,
Whom I have begotten out of [my loins],
24. Thutmes, who lives for evermore,
Who has shown all love to my Being.
Thou hast raised my dwelling in long-lasting works
More extensive and broader than they have ever been-
A great gate [protects against the entrance of the impious].
25. Thou hast established joyful feasts in favor of Amon.
Greater are thy monuments than those of all former kings.
I gave thee the order to execute them,
And thou hast understood it.
Therefore I place thee on the chair of Hor for never-ending many years.
Conduct and guide the living generations!"

The foregoing song of victory of the unknown Theban poet, the similar songs of victory in honor of the kings Ramses II. and III., the heroic song of the poet Pentaur on the great deeds of king Ramses II. during his campaign against the king of Kadesh and his allies, will remain for all times unequalled specimens of the old Egyptian language at its highest epoch.

The victories of the heroic king Thutmes III., who during his numerous campaigns brought the lands and cities of western Asia into his power, to

THE EXODUS OF ISRAEL. 147

whom Libya and the peoples of Nubia and Ethiopia, as far as the promontory now called Gardafui opposite the south coast of Arabia, were subject, — had brought to Egypt unnumbered prisoners of every race, who, according to the old custom, found their fit occupation in the public works. It was principally to the great public edifices, and among these especially to the enlarged buildings of the temple of Amon, at Ape (near Karnak), that the foreigners were forced to devote all their labor, under the superintendence of the Egyptian architects (Mer) and overseers (Rois), who had on their part to carry out the orders and directions of the royal head architect. In those days a certain Puam was clothed with this high office at the court of pharaoh; his name is of Semitic origin, meaning 'one who has the mouth full of dinner.' The prisoners were obliged, in a manner answering to their condition, to undergo the severest labors at the buildings. To these belonged especially the baking of the bricks, as it is portrayed in so clear and lively a manner in the Book of Books in the description of the oppression of the children of Israel in Egypt.

Fate has preserved to us on the walls of a chamber in a tomb in the interior of the hill of Abd-el-Qurnah, in the region of the melancholy 'coffin-hill'

(Du-neb-ankh), a very instructive pictorial representation, in which the pencil of the deceased master has portrayed in lively colors to future generations the industry of the prisoners. Far more convincing than the explanations, written by the side in old Egyptian letters and words, these curious drawings themselves allow us to recognize to their full extent the fate and the severe labor of the unfortunate prisoners. Some carry water in jugs from the tank hard by; others knead and cut up the loamy earth; others again, by the help of a wooden form, make the bricks, or place them carefully in long rows to dry; while the more intelligent among them carry out the work of building the walls. The words which are added as explanations of each occupation give us the authentic information that the laborers are captive people which Thutmes III. has carried away to build the temple of his father Amon. They explain that the 'baking of the bricks' is a work for the new building of the provision-house of the god Amon, of Apet (the east side of Thebes); and they finally declare, in a copious manner, the strict superintendence of the steward over the foreigners in the following words: " (Here are seen) the prisoners which have been carried away as living prisoners in very great numbers; they work at the building with active fingers; their overseers

THE EXODUS OF ISRAEL. 149

show themselves in sight; these insist with vehemence, obeying the orders of the great skilled Lord (who prescribes to them) the works, and gives dircetions to the masters; (they are rewarded) with wine and all kinds of good dishes; they perform their service with a mind full of love for the king; they build for Thutmes III. a Holy of Holies for (the gods), may it be rewarded to him through a range of many years."

The overseer (Rois) speaks thus to the laborers at the building: 'The stick is in my hand, be not idle.'

The picture and the words, which we have laid before our readers exactly as they have been transmitted to us, present an important illustration of the accounts in the Bible concerning the hard bondage of the Jews in Egypt. We also there read, 'And they set overseers over them, who oppressed them with hard servitude, for they built for pharaoh the towns of Pithom and Raamses as treasure-cities.' 'And they made their life hard to them with severe work in clay and brick.' 'And the overseers urged them and said, Fulfil your day's work.'

The severe and continuous labor so represented was bestowed upon the various great temples at Thebes; among them was the Sekhem, or Holy of Holies of the god Amon, and the stupendous Hall of Pillars, called Khu-menuu, or 'splendid memorial,' which was dedicated not only to the god Amon, but also to the deified rulers, whom Thutmes III. acknowledged as his legitimate predecessors on the throne, and as the ancestors of his own house. Here, in one of the chambers situated towards the south, was found that celebrated wall of the kings which is known to science under the designation of the Table of Kings of Karnak. In this the pharaoh traces back his pedigree to his great ancestor Senoferu, of the third dynasty (of Memphis), and reckons the kings Assa, Pepi, the petty kings of the name of Antef, the famous sovereigns of the twelfth dynasty, and some thirty princes of the thirteenth, as his ancestors.

The great southern propylæa of the temple have suffered much from the corroding tooth of time and the destroying hand of man. But even the remains which have survived, a heap of lonely ruins, enable us to judge of the high perfection of the artistic powers, which created such almost unrivalled masterworks, and were able, by means to us inexplicable, to overcome the resistance of the hardest stone. Whether we suffer our attention to dwell on the way in which these great masses of stone have been brought together and united in a complete structure perfectly well arranged and producing the effect of symmetry alike in the whole and in the several parts; whether we feast our sight upon the marvellous ornamental work in stone, by means of which the artist's hand had the skill to delight us with a welcome interruption of the great plain surfaces; whether we gaze with astonished eyes upon the indescribable dignity and the kingly mien of the remaining statues of standing or sitting pharaohs and deities; whether, in fine, we admire the sharp cutting and the dexterity, never after attained, in the drawing of the hieroglyphics, which in long lines and columns cover walls, pillars, and sculptures, rather as ornaments than inscriptions: wherever we turn, there presents itself to us — the late heirs to that long-buried world of old — that sixteenth century before our era, the age of the Thutmes and their immediate successors, as the most perfect acmé of the old Egyptian art, as grand in its conception of the whole, as it was full of taste and refinement in the execution of the several parts.

Dr. Brugsch devotes a large space to the various edifices, obelisks, and statues which have been identified by himself and others as the work of this great king, and which show that his care was co-extensive with his dominion. In Nubia and in the island of Elephantine, in ancient Memphis, in various cities in the north, and even in far Mesopotamia, the evidences of his power have been found.

We will here bid farewell to the greatest king of Egyptian history; the victorious conqueror and ruler of a whole world, from the southernmost lands of inner Africa to the columns of heaven in the land of Naharain; to the founder of a multitude of new temples, to the upholder of the temples of his forefathers, to the celebrated benefactor of the servants of the gods, to whom, during a long existence, it was granted by the divine ones to see perpetuated on their temple walls the deeds of his arm and the achievements of his genius. What wonder then that his contemporaries already worshipped him while alive as a divine being, and allotted to him after his death the honors of an inhabitant of heaven? His name was inscribed on thousands of little images, and small stone scarabæi, which were used for rings; he was considered as the luck-bringing god of the country, and a preserver against the evil influence of wicked spirits and magicians.

Thus the memory of the king has lasted to our days; and it is not by accident that even the sons of Europe and America, whom a love of knowledge and curiosity, or the mild air of the Egyptian heaven, leads to the blessed shores of the Nile, of all the pharaohs, first learn the name of Ra-men-kheper, which Thutmes III. bore in his cartouche.

CHAPTER IX.

AMENHOTEP III., AND KHUNATEN, THE HERETIC.

THE great Thutmes was succeeded by Amenhotep II., and by Thutmes IV., both vigorous and renowned kings. The next in the line, however, Amenhotep III., was far more illustrious. There exists a famous memorial of this monarch in the form of a pair of immense statues in sitting posture, of which, fortunately, there is an authentic account written by the sculptor himself. His name, like that of the king, was Amenhotep.

"My lord promoted me to be the chief architect. I immortalized the name of the king, and no one has done the like of me in my works, reckoning from early times. For him was created the sand-stone hill; he is indeed the heir of the god Toom. I acted according to what seemed best in my estimation, inasmuch as I executed two portrait-statues of noble hard stone in this his great building. It equals heaven. No king has done the like since the time of the reign of the Sun-god Ra, who possessed the land. Thus I executed these works of art, his statues — (they were astonishing for their breadth, and height in a perpendicular direction: their completed form made the propylon look small; 40 cubits was their measure) — in the splendid sand-stone mountain,* on its two sides, that of Ra and that of Toom (that is, the east and west sides).

"I caused to be built eight ships; they (the statues) were carried up (the river) and placed in their sublime building. They will last as long as heaven.

"I declare to you who shall come here after us, that of the people who were assembled for the building, every one was under me. They were full of ardor; their heart was moved with joy; they raised a shout and praised the gracious god. Their landing in Thebes was a joyful event. The monuments were raised in their future place."

We must not fail here to remark to our readers, that the statues of the king, of forty cubits high (that is, twenty-one metres, or nearly seventy English feet), mentioned in the inscription, are the two celebrated statues of Memnon, about which we shall speak presently. The measure assigned to them answers to the modern measurements,† and so does the

---

* Perhaps the quarries of Silsilis are here meant, which in fact lie on the east and west sides of the river, and the inscriptions of which refer to these works.

† According to actual measurement, the height of the sitting figures, from the crown of the head to the sole of the feet, is 14·28 metres, not counting the destroyed head-dress. The footstool has a height of 4·25 metres. The whole height of the statues, with the foundation, is 18·53 metres. According to the above inscription, which gives the whole a height of 21 metres. the head-dress must be reckoned at 2·47 metres, which answers exactly to the height of a so-called pshent-crown.

description of their size, which must have made the tower gateway (propylon) which stood behind them look small. Thus, thanks to a peculiar ordering of destiny, which has preserved to us his own statues, we now know the noble lord and master who conceived the plan of this double gigantic work, the size and extent of which has excited the greatest astonishment and unqualified admiration of the ancients as well as the moderns. It was the head architect, Amenhotep, the son of Hapoo, who had the skill to create them in the sandstone quarries of Silsilis, besides building the temple.

On the further bank of the river, in a north-easterly direction from the temple of Thutmes III., in Medinet Abu, a new temple to the god Amon was raised by the king's command. Its site is indicated from a great distance by the gigantic sitting statues of the king, the fame of which the ancients spread over the whole world, under the name of the Statues of Memnon. Although little more than the foundation-walls of the temple itself are left, yet a memorial tablet, which now lies thrown down on its back, bears witness to the size and importance of the original building. In the inscription which adorns its surface, there is described a dialogue between the king and the god. First the king, Amenhotep III., speaks thus:

"Come then, Amon-Ra, lord of Thebes in Ape, behold thy dwelling, which is prepared for thee on the great place of Us (Thebes); thy glory resides in the western part (of the city). Thou passest through the heaven to unite thyself with her (the city), and thou risest on the circle of heaven (in the east); then is she enlightened by the golden beams of thy countenance. Her front turns towards the east, &c.

"Thy glory dwells in her. I have not let her want for excellent works of lasting beautiful white stone. I have filled her with monuments in my (name), from the hill of the wonderful stones. Those who show them in their place are full of great joy on account of their size."

The temple, now in ruins, was carried out according to the plan of the chief architect, the same who boasts of having designed the two gigantic statues of the king in front of it.

These rise, at the present day, like two solitary watchers with the heaps of ruins at their backs, on the cultivated Theban plain, reached every year by the water of the inundation, which often moistens their rigid feet.

The two statues — which represent king Amenhotep in a sitting position, having at their feet small sitting statues of his wife Thi, and of his mother, Mut-em-ua — are carved each out of a single block of a firm red-brown sandstone, mixed with pieces of white quartz, and are in fact marvellous productions of treatment in the hardest and most brittle material. They stand at a distance of twenty-two feet from one another. The northern one is that which the Greeks and Romans celebrated in poetry and prose by the name of the vocal statue of Memnon. Its legs are covered with the inscriptions of Greek, Roman, Phœnician, and Egyptian travellers, written to assure the reader that they had really visited the place, or had heard the musical tones of Memnon at the rising of the sun.

In the year 27 B. C., in consequence of an earthquake, the whole of the upper part of the statue was removed from its place and thrown to the ground. From that time, the tourists of antiquity began to immortalize themselves by scratching their names, and adding befitting or unbefitting remarks. The assurances that they had heard Memnon sing, or rather ring (or tinkle), end under the reign of the emperor Septimius Severus, who completed the wanting upper part of the body as well as he could with blocks of stone piled up and fastened together. It is a well-known fact, of which that immortal master of science, Alexander von Humboldt, personally assured me, that split or cracked rocks, or stone walls, after cooling during the night, at the rising of the sun, as soon as the stone becomes warmed, emit a prolonged ringing (or tinkling) note. The sudden change from cold to heat creates quick currents of air, which press through the crevices of the rock, and emit a peculiar melancholy singing tone. When, in the year 1851, I chose as my dwelling for some months the temple of Ape, to the west of the temple of Khonsu at Karnak, I heard of a morning, after the sun had been some time up in the heaven, from a side chamber warmed by it, a melancholy note like that of the vocal Memnon. The fact was so well known to the Arabs who lived there, that they showed me this very chamber as that where the death-watch struck. After the statue of Memnon had been restored in the manner I have described, the sound naturally ceased of itself. The crack in the sandstone was covered by the masonry which was built up over it.

The historical legend of the vocal Memnon is thus a very modern story, about which the old Egyptians knew nothing. The song of Memnon, however poetical it may have been in the fancy of antiquity, must be at once struck out of the history of Egypt. In its place the dry narrative of the Greek historian Pausanias resumes its full right, according to which the statue was that of a man of the country, by name Phamenoph, that is, 'Amenhotep.' We know now who this Amenhotep was,—

a king of that name, who, in spite of himself, was made the Memnon of the Greek fable.

The architect Amenhotep, the son of Hapoo, who had the ability to execute so great a work, deserves so much the more the honor of having his name perpetuated, as he independently and without any order from the king, conceived so grand a plan and carried it out successfully. It was not only necessary to loosen the stone from the rocks and work it, but also to entrust the vast weight to the Nile, and to convey it from the Theban riverbank to its proper position. He was obliged, as he himself tells us, to build eight ships, in order to carry the burden of these gigantic statues. Even in our highly cultivated age, with all its inventions and machines, which enable us by the help of steam to raise and transport the heaviest weights, the shipment and erection of the statues of Memnon remain to us an insoluble riddle. Verily Amenhotep, the son of Hapoo, must have been not only a wise, but a specially ingenious man of his time.

Amenhotep IV., who afterwards adopted the surname of Khu-n-aten, had a singular origin and history. He stands alone, the solitary heretic king. According to the laws of descent, he was not in the direct line, because his father had by a misalliance passed over the hereditary princesses of the royal race. The priests of Amon never recognized him as a lawful ruler, and their hostility to him was increased by his aversion to the worship of Amon, the greatly venerated god of Egypt.

In the house of his mother Thi, the daughter of the foreigner, beloved by his father, hated by the priests, the young prince had willingly received the teaching about the one God of Light; and what the mouth of his mother had impressed upon his childish mind in tender youth became a firm faith when he arrived at man's estate. The king was so little prepared to renounce the new doctrine, that he designated himself within the royal cartouche itself as 'a high-priest of Hormakhu,' and 'a friend of the sun's disk,' Mi-aten. Such a heresy in the orthodox city of Amon, full of temples, was at once deemed an unheard-of thing; and open hate soon took the place of the aversion which had existed from the first. To the great misfortune of the king himself, his outward appearance betrayed, in a very unpleasing manner, his descent from his foreign mother.

To fill up the measure of hatred against the caste of the priests of Amon, and to give it public expression, the king issued a command to obliterate the names of Amon and of his wife Mut from the monuments of his royal ancestors. Hammer and chisel were put in active requisition on the engraved stones, and the scribes of the royal court sought with care the places, even to the very names of his forefathers, in which the word Amon met the reader's eye.

The discontent of the priests and the people had reached its highest point, and open rebellion broke out against the heretic king, who, ashamed of his honorable baptismal name of Amenhotep, had assumed the new name Khunaten, that is, 'splendor of the sun's disk,' by which we must henceforward designate him.

The king, under the conviction that he could not any longer remain in the city of Amon, determined to turn his back on the cradle of his ancestors, and to found a new capital, which he called Khu-aten, far from Memphis and Thebes, at a place in middle Egypt, which at this day bears the name of Tell-el-Amarna.

Artists, overseers, and workmen were summoned with hot haste. According to the plans of the king, a splendid temple was erected in hard stone, in honor of the sun-god Aten, composed of many buildings, and with open courts, in which fire-altars were set up. The plan of the great building was new, with little of the Egyptian character, and arranged in a peculiar manner.

As the chief official who was set over the king's house, there lived at the court of this pharaoh a certain Aahmes, who also had the superintendence of the provision-houses of the temple. Next to Meri-ra, he was one of the most zealous adherents of the new teaching. His prayer to the Sun, which is preserved to us among the sepulchral inscriptions at Tell-el-Amarna, will confirm this:

"Beautiful is thy setting, thou Sun's disk of life, thou lord of lords, and king of the worlds. When thou unitest thyself with the heaven at thy setting, mortals rejoice before thy countenance, and give honor to him who has created them, and pray before him who has formed them, before the glance of thy son, who loves thee, the King Khunaten. The whole land of Egypt and all peoples repeat all thy names at thy rising, to magnify thy rising in like manner as thy setting. Thou, O God, who in truth art the living one, standest before the two eyes. Thou art he which createst what never was, which formest everything, which art in all things; we also have come into being through the word of thy mouth.

"Give me favor before the king forever; let there not be wanting to me a peaceful burial after attaining old age in the land of Khu-aten, when I shall have finished my course of life in a good state.

"I am a servant of the divine benefactor (that is of the king), I accompany him to all places where he loves to dwell. I am his companion at his feet. For he raised me to greatness when I was yet a child, till [the day of my] honor in good fortune. The servant of the prince rejoices, and is in a festive disposition every day."

THE EXODUS OF ISRAEL. 163

In these and similar creations of a poetic form there reigns such a depth of view, and so devout a conception of God, that we are almost inclined to give our complete assent to the teaching, about which the king is wont to speak so fully and with so much pleasure.

His royal spouse also, Nofer-i-Thi, was deeply penetrated with the exalted doctrines of the new faith, which to contemporaries appeared in the light of an open heresy against the mysterious traditions on the being of the godhead in the rolls of the holy books of the other temples of the land.

According to the wall-pictures in two sepulchral chambers in the hills behind the town, the pharaoh Khunaten enjoyed a very happy family life. Surrounded by his daughters and wife, who often, from a high balcony, threw down all kinds of presents to the crowd which stood below, the mother holding on her lap the little Ankh-nes-aten, — he reached a state of the highest enjoyment, and found in the love of his family, and the devout adoration of his god, indemnification for the loss of the attachment of the 'holy fathers' and of a great part of the people. The widowed queen-mother Thi also shared this family happiness, and thus we find her sitting in peaceful intercourse with her son and his wife, in the hall of the royal palace.

King Khunaten gave remarkable expression to his love for his relations by three rock pictures, with inscriptions all to the same effect, which remain on the steep face of the rock near the city of Khu-aten, but are barely within reach of the eye. The king and queen are seen in the upper compartment, raising their hands in an attitude of prayer to the god of light, whose disk rises over their heads in the full splendor of his beams, each ray of the sun terminating in a hand dispensing life. Two daughters, Meri-aten and Mak-aten, accompany their royal parents.

Here is one paragraph of the inscription:

"Thereupon King Khunaten swore an oath to his father thus: Sweet love fills my heart for the queen, for her young children. Grant a great age to the Queen Nofri-Thi in long years; may she keep the hand of Pharaoh. Grant a great age to the royal daughter Meri-aten, and to the royal daughter Mak-aten, and to their children; may they keep the hand of the queen, their mother, eternally and forever."

This memorial, in the form of a rock tablet, remains to this day.

King Khunaten died without male issue, — possibly by violence, — and his three sons-in-law in turn succeeded him upon the throne. But neither of them had the favor of the priests, and their hold upon the supreme power was short. A certain Ai, who had been master of the horse under king Khunaten, seized upon the empire; and, as he brought back the worship to the old temples and reinstated the old priests in power, he had a prosperous reign, and went through the usual campaigns against the neighbors of Egypt. During his reign all possible damage was inflicted upon the works of the monotheist king Khunaten, with the intent to blot out his name from the earth. Ai was succeeded by Horemhib, or Horus, who had no shadow of title, except that his wife was sister to a former queen. His reign seems to have been more than ordinarily brilliant; and full particulars of his coronation and memorials of his deeds are preserved in a papyrus preserved at Turin, of which Dr. Brugsch gives a full and stately translation.

We give the concluding portion. The gods of Egypt are represented as having assembled to welcome and to crown the new pharaoh:

" Then came forth from the palace the holiness of this splendid god Amon, the king of the gods, with his son before him, and he embraced his pleasant form, which was crowned with the royal helmet, in order to deliver to him the golden protecting image of the sun's disk. The nine foreign nations were under his feet, the heaven was in festive disposition, the land was filled with ecstasy, and as for the divinities of Egypt, their souls were full of pleasant feelings. Then the inhabitants, in high delight, raised towards heaven the song of praise; great and small lifted up their voices, and the whole land was moved with joy.

"After this festival in Ape of the southern country was finished, then went Amon, the king of the gods, in peace to Thebes, and the king went down the river on board of his ship, like an image of Hormakhu. Thus had he taken possession of this land, as was the custom since the time of the sun-god Ra. He renewed the dwellings of the gods, from the shallows of the marsh-land of Nathu as far as Nubia. He had all their images sculptured, each as it had been before, more than . . . And the sun-god Ra rejoiced, when he beheld (that renewed) which in former times had been destroyed. He set them up in their temple, and he had a hundred images made, one for each of them, of like form, and of all kinds of costly stones. He visited the cities of the gods, which lay as heaps of rubbish in this land, and he had them restored just as they had been from the beginning of all things. He took care for their daily festival of sacrifice, and for all the vessels of their temples, formed out of gold and silver. He provided them (the temples) with holy persons and singers, and with the best of the body-guards; and he presented to them arable land and cattle, and supplied them with all kinds of provisions which they required, to sing thus each new morning to the sun-god Ra: 'Thou hast made the kingdom great for us in thy son, who is the consolation of thy soul, king Horemhib. Grant him the continuance of the thirty years' feasts, give him the victory over all countries, as to Hor, the son of Isis, towards whom in like manner thy heart yearned in On,* in the company of thy circle of gods.'"

* Heliopolis.

CHAPTER X.

THE PHARAOH OF THE OPPRESSION.

THE nineteenth dynasty began with Ramses I., a monarch of little renown. He was succeeded by his son Mineptah I., Seti I., commonly known as Seti, a famous warrior, who pushed his armies in every direction and inflicted the severest punishment upon every nation that resisted. The weight of his wrath fell upon the unhappy Canaanites and the Shasu (ancestors of the modern Arabs). A contemporary record says: " His joy is to undertake the battle, and his delight is to dash into it. His heart is only satisfied at the sight of the stream of blood when he strikes off the heads of his enemies. A moment of the struggle of men is dearer to him than a day of pleasure. He slays them with one stroke, and spares none among them."

He carried his victorious arms to Mount Lebanon, and when he returned to Egypt brought numbers of tall cedars for masts, and for flagstaffs to adorn Theban temples.

The buildings erected in this reign, especially the

temples, are grand specimens of the art. These concessions to the priests, however, did not in their estimation counterbalance the injury done to the national religion by the king's worship of foreign deities. He was wholly devoted to the service of the Canaanitish god Baal (so often mentioned in Scripture), whose second name, Set, was reproduced in his own, Seti.

When his son Ramses II. was twelve years old he was associated with his father in the government; and his reign extended to not less than sixty-seven years, so that he was nearly eighty years of age at the time of his death.

Ramses II. is sometimes called Ramses Miamun, and one of the royal prefixes is Soter-en-ra.

This is the king who above all others bears the name of honor of A-nakhtu, 'the Conqueror,' and whom the monuments and the rolls of the books often designate by his popular names of Ses, Sestesu, Setesu, or Sestura, that is, the 'Sethosis, who is also called Ramesses' of the Manethonian record, and the renowned legendary conqueror Sesostris of the Greek historians.

The number of his monuments, which still to the present day cover the soil of Egypt and Nubia in almost countless numbers, as the ruined remnants of a glorious past, or are daily brought to light from their concealment, is so great and almost countless, that the historian of his life and deeds finds himself in a difficulty where to begin, how to spin together the principal threads, and where to end his work.

The first care of Ramses after his father's death was to restore the dilapidated temples and public buildings, to set up statues, and to engrave lasting memorials of his ancestors, not forgetting his own extraordinary merits. On the wall of a temple at Abydus is still to be seen an inscription, of which the translation occupies over eight closely printed octavo pages. This is wholly occupied with an account of the great works done by the king in the restoration of ancient edifices and in brightening the records of history. The style is ornate and at times poetical, full of figures and of bold apostrophes, and at the same time wonderfully like that of the biblical writers. But Ramses appears to have been a boaster, and his real works are far inferior to those of his father, the ferocious Seti.

It is scarcely worth while to relate what Ramses II. did for the buildings of his father at Abydus. In the course of his long reign the king completed the temple. When the great building was finished, he must have been advanced in years, since not less than sixty sons and fifty-nine daughters greeted in their pictures the entrance of the pilgrims at the principal gate. In proportion as the works executed under Seti, the father, present to the astonished eyes of the beholder splendid examples of Egyptian architecture and sculpture, just so poor and inferior are the buildings which were executed under the reign of Ramses, and which bear the names of the Conquering King. The feeling also of gratitude towards his parent seems to have gradnally faded away with Ramses, as years increased upon him, to such a degree, that he did not even deem it wrong to chisel out the names and memorials of his father in many places of the temple walls, and to substitute his own.

Ramses IL, like most of his predecessors, carried on foreign wars, especially against the Khita or inhabitants of Canaan. He obtained a doubtful victory over them at Kadesh; and as he came out of the fight alone, and preserved his life by his personal bravery, the event was celebrated in the most extravagant manner. The long and boastful accounts of this action and of the campaign were sculptured upon temple walls, and were illustrated by battle-scènes containing multitudes of figures, including, of course, the *effigies* of the conqueror himself. These vast pictured tablets are among the most valuable of historical monuments. The same exploit was made the occasion of a long heroic poem, the earliest of war lyrics preserved to us.

The temple-scribe, Penta-ur, a jovial companion, who, to the special disgust of his old teacher, manifested a decided inclination for wine, women, and song, had the honor, in the seventh year of Ramses IL, to win the prize as the composer of an heroic song, a copy of which we not only possess in a roll of papyrus, but its words cover the whole surface of walls in the temples of Abydus,* Luqsor, Karnak, the Ramesseum at Ibsambool, in order to call the attention of the visitor, even at a distance, to the deeds of Ramses.

The fact that it was engraved on the temple walls, and on the hard stone, may serve as a proof of the recognition which was accorded to the poet by the king and his contemporaries. And, indeed, even our own age will hardly refuse to applaud this work, although a translation cannot reach the power and beauty of the original. Throughout the poem the peculiar cast of thought of the Egyptian poet fourteen centuries before Christ continually shines out in all its fulness, and confirms our opinion, that the Mosaic language exhibits to us an exact counterpart of the Egyptian mode of speech.

* The parts of this temple which were dug out have been again carefully covered up with sand.

THE EXODUS OF ISRAEL. 173

The whole substance of thought of minds living at the same time, and in society with each other, must needs have tended towards the same conception and form, even though the idea which the one had of God was essentially different from the views of the other concerning the nature of the Creator of all things.

From the poet we pass to the unknown painter and sculptor, who has chiselled in deep work on the stone of the same wall, with a bold execution of the several parts, the procession of the warriors, the battle before Kadesh, the storming of the fortress, the overthrow of the enemy, and the camp life of the Egyptians. The whole conception must even at this day be acknowledged to be grand beyond measure, for the representation sets before our eyes the deeds which were performed more vividly than any description in words and with the richest handling of the material, and displays the whole composition even to its smallest details.

The poem of Penta-ur (Penta the Great) is doubtless full of fire, and is a priceless relic; but it is too long for the limits of this work, and no satisfactory abridgment could be made of it. The song of triumph attributed to Moses in the book of Exodus came a generation later.

After a long war, a peace was made at the city of

Ramses,* between the two most powerful nations of the world at that time, Khita in the east, and Kemi in the west. It was to be hoped that the new offensive and defensive alliance, which united the princes and countries in the manner thus described, would attain its end, and bridle the fermenting restless world of the people of the Canaanites, which lay between them, and keep down every rising and movement of the hostilely disposed Semites, and confine them within the limits once for all fixed. For that a ferment existed, even in the inmost heart of the Egyptian land, is sufficiently proved by the allusion in the treaty to the evasions of evil-disposed subjects. We may perhaps read between the lines that the Jewish people are meant, who, since their migration into the land of Egypt, had increased beyond measure, and without doubt were already making preparations to withdraw themselves from the power of their oppressors on the banks of the Nile. But how? and when? — this was hidden in the councils of the Eternal.

Although Ramses raised his monuments in Thebes, and went up to the old capital of the empire to cele-

* The ancient name of the city was Zoan, often written Zoan-Tanis, because situate in the Tanitic nome. When Ramses II. made it the royal residence it was called Pi-Ramses (city of Ramses), or sometimes Zoan-Ramses. It is called in the book of Exodus Raamses.

brate the festival of Amon; although he held public courts in Memphis, to take counsel about the goldfields in the Nubian country; although he visited Abydus, to see the tombs of the kings and the temple of the dead built by his father;—not to mention Heliopolis, in which he dedicated a temple and obelisks to the sun-god;—yet neither these nor other cities formed his permanent abode. On the eastern frontier of Egypt, in the lowlands of the Delta, in Zoan-Tanis, was the proper royal residence of the pharaoh.

We have often mentioned this city, and have come to understand its important position. Connected with the sea, being situated on the then broad and navigable Tanitic arm of the Nile, it commanded also the entrance of the great road, covered by 'Khetams,' or fortresses, which led to Palestine either in a north-easterly direction through Pelusium, or in an easterly direction through Migdol, on the royal road. Zoan-Tanis was, in the proper sense of the word, *the key of Egypt*. Impressed with the importance of the position of this 'great city,' Ramessu transferred his court to Zoan, strengthened its fortifications, and founded a new temple-city.

The hieratic rolls of papyrus, which have outlived the ravages of time, with one voice designate the newly founded temple-city (for the kings of the eighteenth dynasty had quite abandoned the old Zoan) as the central point of the court history of Egypt. Here resided the scribes, who in their letters have left behind for us the manifold information which the life at the court, the ordinances of the king and of the chief officials, and their relations with their families in the most distant parts of the country, required them to give without reserve. Zoan, or, as the place is henceforth called, Pi-Ramessu, 'the city of Ramses,' became henceforward the especial capital of the empire.

It will be useful to the reader to hear in what manner an Egyptian letter-writer described the importance of this town on the occasion of his visit to it:

"So I arrived in the city of Ramses-Miamun, and I have found it excellent, for nothing can compare with it on the Theban land and soil. (Here is the seat) of the court. It is pleasant to live in. Its fields are full of good things, and life passes in constant plenty and abundance. Its canals are rich in fish, its lakes swarm with birds, its meadows are green with vegetables, there is no end of the lentils; melons with a taste like honey grow in the irrigated fields. Its barns are full of wheat and durra, and reach as high as heaven. Onions and sesame are in the enclosures, and the apple-tree blooms. (?) The vine, the almond-tree, and the fig-tree grow in the gardens. Sweet is their wine for the inhabitants of Kemi. They mix it with honey. The red fish is in the lotus-canal, the Borian-fish in the ponds, many kinds of Bori-fish, besides carp and pike, in the canal of Pu-barotha; fat fish and Khipti-pennu fish are in the pools of the inundation, the Hauaz-fish in the full mouth of the Nile, near the 'city of the conqueror' (Tanis). The city-canal Pshenhor produces salt, the lake region of Pahir natron. Their sea-ships enter the harbor, plenty and abundance is perpetual in it. He rejoices who has settled there. My information is no jest. The common people, as well as the higher classes, say, 'Come hither! let us celebrate to him his heavenly and his earthly feasts.' The inhabitants of the reedy lake (Thufi) arrived with lilies, those of Pshensor with papyrus flowers. Fruits from the nurseries, flowers from the gardens, birds from the ponds, are dedicated to him. Those who dwell near the sea came with fish, and the inhabitants of their lakes honored him. The youths of the 'Conqueror's city' were perpetually clad in festive attire. Fine oil was on their heads of fresh-curled hair. They stood at their doors, their hands laden with branches and flowers from Pahathor, and with garlands from Pahir, on the day of the entry of king Ramessu-Miamun, the god of war Monthu upon earth, in the early morning of the monthly feast of Kihith (that is, on the 1st of Khoiakh). All people were assembled, neighbor with neighbor, to bring forward their complaints.

"Delicious was the wine for the inhabitants of the 'Conqueror's city.' Their cider was like . . . . , their sherbets were like almonds mixed with honey. There was beer from Kati (Galilee) in the harbor, wine in the gardens, fine oil at the lake Sagabi, garlands in the apple-orchards. The sweet song of women resounded to the tunes of Memphis. So they sat there with joyful heart, or walked about without ceasing. King Ramessu-Miamun, he was the god they celebrated."

In spite of the unexplained names of the fishes and plants, the scribe could hardly have given a clearer or livelier account of the impression made on his susceptible mind by the new city of Ramses in its festal garments on the day of the entry of pharaoh. We may suppose that many a Hebrew, perhaps Moses himself, jostled the Egyptian scribe in his wandering through the gaily dressed streets of the temple-city.

And this city of Ramses is the very same which is named in Holy Scripture as one of the two places in which pharaoh had built for him 'arei miskenoth,' 'treasure cities,' as the translators understand it.* It would be better, having regard to the actual Egyptian word 'mesket,' 'meskenet,' 'temple, holy place' (as, for example, king Darius designates his temple erected in the great Oasis to the Theban Amon), to translate it 'temple-cities.' The new pharaoh, 'who knew not Joseph,'† who adorned the city of Ramses, the capital of the Tanitic nome, and the city of Pithom, the capital of what was afterwards the Sethroitic nome, with temple-cities, is no other, *can be no other*, than Ramessu II., of whose

* Exod. i. 13: "And they built for Pharaoh treasure cities, Pithom and Raamses."

† Who did not recognize what Joseph had long before done for Egypt.

buildings at Zoan the monuments and the papyrus-rolls speak in complete agreement. And although, as it happens, Pitum is not named as a city in which Ramses erected new temples to the local divinities, the fact is all the more certain, that Zoan contained a new city of Ramses, the great temple-district of the newly founded sanctuaries of the above-named gods. Ramessu is the pharaoh of the oppression, and the father of that unnamed princess who found the child Moses exposed in the bulrushes on the bank of the river.

While the fact, that the pharaoh we have named was the founder of the city of Ramses, is so strongly demonstrated by the evidence of the Egyptian records both on stone and papyrus, that only want of intelligence and mental blindness can deny it, the inscriptions do not mention one syllable about the Israelites. We must suppose that the captives were included in the general name of foreigners, of whom the documents make such frequent mention. The hope, however, is not completely excluded, that some hidden papyrus may still give us information about them, as unexpected as it would be welcome.

We must again remark, and insist with strong emphasis on the fact, that from this time, and in the future history of the empire, the town of Zoan-

Tanis is of great importance. On the wide plains before Zoan, the hosts of the warriors were mustered to be exercised in the manœuvres of battle; here the chariots of war rolled by with their stamping pairs of horses; the sea-going ships and their crews came to land at the harbors on the broad river. From this place Thutmes III. had started in his war against western Asia; it was to Tanis that Ramses II. had directed his return from Thebes; here he had received the embassy of peace from the king of Khita; and from hence, as we shall presently have to relate, Moses led the Hebrews out of the land of bondage to the land of promise, to give his people the milk and honey of the Holy Land, in exchange for the flesh-pots of Egypt.

The influx of Semite-Asiatic hostages and prisoners exercised a continually increasing influence on religion, manners, and language. The Egyptian language was enriched (we might almost say, for our profit) with foreign expressions, often indeed from mere whim, but more often for good reasons, in order properly to designate unknown objects by their native names. The letters and documents of the time of the Ramessids are full of Semitic words thus introduced, and in this respect they are scarcely less affected· than the German language now, the strength and beauty of which are so much degraded by the borrowing of outlandish words.

Ramses II. enjoyed a long reign. The monuments expressly testify to a rule of sixty-seven years, of which probably more than half must be assigned to his joint reign with his father. Great in war, and active in the works of peace, Ramses seems also to have enjoyed the richest blessings of heaven in his family life. The outer wall of the front of the temple of Abydus gives us the pictures and the names (only partially preserved) of 119 children (59 sons and 60 daughters).

The elder sons died during the long reign of their father. The fourteenth in the long list of children, by name Mineptah, 'the friend of Ptah,' was chosen by destiny to mount at last the throne of the pharaohs. He had already taken part in the affairs of government during the lifetime of his aged father, and in this capacity he appears on the monuments of Ramses II., by the side of his royal parent.

Of the daughters of the king, the monuments name, during the lifetime of the pharaoh, as real queens and wives of Egyptian kings (perhaps sub-kings or brothers), his favorite daughter, called by the Semitic name of Bint-antha, 'the daughter of Anaitis,' and Meri-amon, and Neb-taui. A much younger sister of the name of Meri (Dear) deserves to be mentioned, since her name reminds us of the Princess Merris (also called Thermuthis), according to the Jewish tradition,* who found the child Moses on the bank of the stream, when she went to bathe. Is it by accident, or by divine providence, that in the reign of Ramses III., about one hundred years after the death of his ancestor, the great Sesostris, a place is mentioned in Middle Egypt, which bears the name of the great Jewish legislator? It is called T-en-Moshé, 'the island of Moses,' or 'the river-bank of Moses.' It lay on the eastern side of the river, near the city of the heretic king Khu-n-aten.† The place still existed in the time of the Romans; those who describe Egypt at that time designate it with a mistaken apprehension of its true meaning, as Musai, or Musôn, as if it had some connection with the Greek Muses.

* Joseph. *Antiq.* ii. 9, § 35; Artapanus, *ap.* Euseb. *Præp Evang.* ix. 27.
† See p. 161.

CHAPTER XI.

THE PHARAOH OF THE EXODUS AND A SUMMARY OF SUCCEEDING HISTORY.

MINEPTAH II. makes but an insignificant figure among the proud kings of Egypt, being neither renowned for arts nor arms, and being remembered as a weak, cowardly, and cruel ruler. He does not rank with those pharaohs who have transmitted their remembrance to posterity by grand buildings and the construction of new temples, or by the enlargement of such as already existed. With the exception of small portions, hardly worthy of being named, the new pharaoh contented himself with the cheap glory of utilizing, or rather misusing, the monuments of his predecessors, as far back as the twelfth dynasty, and not excepting even the works of the Hyksos, as bearers of his royal shields; for in the cartouches of former kings, whence he had chiselled out their names, he unsernpulously inserted his own, without any respect for the judgment of posterity. The nomad tribes of the Edomite Shasu — who under Seti I. still regarded the eastern region of the Delta, up to the neighborhood of Zoan, the city of Ramses, as their own possession, until they were driven out by that pharaoh over the eastern frontier — bestirred themselves anew under Mineptah, but now in a manner alike peaceful and loyal. As faithful subjects of pharaoh, they asked for a passage through the border fortress of Khetam, in the land of Thuku (Sukoth), in order to find sustenance for themselves and their herds in the rich pasture lands of the lake district about the city of Pitom.

On this subject an Egyptian official makes the following report:

"Another matter for the satisfaction of my master's heart. We have carried into effect the passage of the tribes of the Shasu from the land of Aduma (Edom), through the fortress (Khetam) of Mineptah-Hotephima, which is situated in Thuku (Sukoth), to the lakes of the city Pit-um, of Mineptah-Hotephima, which are situated in the land of Thuku, in order to feed themselves and to feed their herds on the possessions of pharaoh, who is there a beneficent sun for all peoples. In the year 8 . . . . Set, I caused them to be conducted, according the list of the . . . . for the . . . . of the other names of the days, on which the fortress (Khetam) of Mineptah-Hotephima is opened for their passage."

If Ramses-Sesostris, the builder of the temple-city of the same name in the territory of Zoan-Tanis, must be regarded beyond all doubt as the pharaoh under whom the Jewish legislator Moses first saw the light, so the chronological relations — having regard to the great age of the two contemporaries, Ramses II. and Moses — demand that Mineptah should in all probability be acknowledged as the pharaoh of the Exodus. He also had his royal seat in the city of Ramses, and seems to have strengthened its fortifications. The Bible speaks of him only under the general name of PHARAOH, that is, under a true Egyptian title, which was becoming more and more frequent at the time now under our notice. PIR-'AO — 'great house, high gate' — is, according to the monuments, the designation of the king of the land of Egypt for the time being. This does not of itself furnish a decisive argument. Only the incidental statement of the Psalmist, that Moses wrought his wonders in the field of Zoan,* carries us back again to those sovereigns, Ramses II. and Mineptah, who were fond of holding their court in Zoan-Ramses.

Some have very recently wished to recognize the Egyptian appellation of the Hebrews in the name of the so-called 'Aper, 'Apura, or 'Aperiu, the Erythræan people in the east of the nome of Heliopolis, in what is known as the 'red country' on the 'red mountain'; and hence they have drawn conclusions which — speaking modestly, according to our knowledge of the monuments — rest on a weak founda-

---

* Psalm lxxviii. 43.

tion. According to the inscriptions, the name of this people appears in connection with the breeding of horses and the art of horsemanship. In an historical narrative of the time of Thutmes III. (unfortunately much obliterated), the 'Apura are named as horsemen, or knights (senen), who mount their horses at the king's command. In another document, of the time of Ramses III., long after the exodus of the Jews from Egypt, two thousand and eighty-three 'Aperiu are introduced, as settlers in Heliopolis, with the words, 'Knights, sons of the kings and noble lords (Marina) of the 'Aper, settled people, who dwell in this place.' Under Ramses IV. we again meet with 'Aper, eight hundred in number, as inhabitants of foreign origin in the district of 'Ani or 'Aini, on the western shore of the Red Sea, in the neighborhood of the modern Suez.

These and similar data completely exclude all thought of the Hebrews, unless one is disposed to have recourse to suppositions and conjectures against the most explicit statements of the biblical records. On the other hand, the hope can scarcely be cherished that we shall ever find on the public monuments — rather let us say in some hidden roll of papyrus — the events, repeated in an Egyptian version, which relate to the exodus of the Jews and the destruction of pharaoh in the Red Sea.

For the record of these events was inseparably connected with the humiliating confession of a divine visitation, to which a patriotic writer at the court of pharaoh would hardly have brought his mind.

Presupposing, then, that Mineptah is to be regarded as the pharaoh of the Exodus, this ruler must have had to endure serious disturbances of all kinds during the time of his reign: — in the west the Libyans, in the east the Hebrews, and — let us at once add — in the south a spirit of rebellion, which declared itself by the insurrection of a rival king of the family of the great Ramses-Sesostris. The events, which form the lamentable close of his rule over Egypt are passed over by the monuments with perfect silence. The dumb tumulus covers the misfortune which was suffered.

In casting a glance over the most eminent contemporaries of this king, we are reminded especially of his viceroy in Egypt, the 'king's son of Kush,' named Mas, — the same who had been invested with this high office in the southern province under Ramses II. His memory has been perpetuated in a rock inscription at Assuan. We may further make mention — instructed by a record in the quarries of Silsilis — of the noble Pinehas, an Egyptian namesake of the Hebrew Phinehas, the son of Eleazar, son of

Aaron. In conclusion, let us not forget the very influential high-priest of Amon, Roi, or Loi, Lui (i. e. Levi), who under Mineptah held the command of the legion of Amon, administered the treasury of Amon, and, according to the custom of the time, was chief architect to pharaoh. To be sure, this must have been an easy office for him, since there was not much building, except perhaps the royal sepulchre, which the drowned pharaoh probably never entered.

Having arrived at the time when the Hebrews began the conquest of Canaan, and were henceforth a separate nation, it will not be expected that from this point anything more than a brief summary of Egyptian affairs will be given. The twentieth dynasty begins with the reign of Ramses III., and ends with that of Ramses XIII. Foreign war is the one unvarying subject that presents itself as we look over the accounts that have been preserved. Ramses III. appears to have conquered Cyprus, Cilicia, and parts of Asia Minor, and he erected in various parts of Egypt and in foreign countries a large number of memorial buildings 'in his name,' called Ramessea. He is known as Rhampsinitus in the history of Herodotus. The remaining princes of the dynasty require no special mention here. Their reigns were in no way remarkable; and toward the

THE EXODUS OF ISRAEL. 189

last the Theban priests had become so influential as to vie with the pharaoh in power. After the death of Ramses XIII. a priest named Hirhor ascended the throne, being the first of the twenty-first dynasty. The descendants of the Ramessu were banished.

Then came an Assyrian invasion under the mighty king Nimrod (Naromath), ostensibly to reinstate the Ramessids, but really to effect a conquest of Egypt. Nimrod died while in Egypt, and was buried at Abydus. His son Shashank (Shishak in the Bible), became king, and fixed his seat at Bubastus. Egypt was at this time virtually an Assyrian province. This portion of Egyptian history was first made known to the world through the discoveries of Dr. Brugsch. The evidence comes from inscriptions on a large granite block found at Abydus. The twenty-second dynasty began with Shashank I. This monarch — the Shishak of the Bible, the Sesonchis of Manetho — has become a conspicuous person in the history of Egypt, in connection with the records of the Jewish monarchy, through his expedition against the kingdom of Judah. It is well known how Jeroboam, the servant of king Solomon, rebelled against the king his master. After the prophet Ahijah had publicly designated him beforehand, as the man best qualified to be the future sovereign, Jeroboam was obliged to save himself from the anger and the snares of the king, and for this reason he fled to Egypt, to the court of Shashanq I.* Recalled after the death of Solomon, he returned to his home, to be elected king of Israel according to the word of the prophet, while the crown of Judah fell to Solomon's son, Rehoboam.† In the fifth year of this latter king's reign, and probably at the instigation of his former guest (Jeroboam), Shashanq made his expedition against the kingdom of Judah, which ended in the capture and pillaging of Jerusalem.‡

This attack of the Egyptian king on the kingdom of Judah and the levitical cities, which the Scripture relates fully and in all its details, has been also handed down to later ages in outline on a wall of the temple of Amon in the Theban Api. On the south external wall, behind the picture of the victories of king Ramessu II., to the east of the room called the Hall of the Bubastids, the spectator beholds the colossal image of the Egyptian sovereign dealing the heavy blows of his victorious club on the captive Jews. The names of the towns and districts, which Shashanq I. conquered in his

---

* 1 Kings xi 26-40.   † 1 Kings xii.; 2 Chron. iii.
‡ 1 Kings xiv. 25-28; 2 Chron. xii.

expedition against Judah, are paraded in long rows, in their Egyptian forms of writing, and frequently with considerable repetitions, each name being enclosed in an embattled shield.

This succession of Assyrian kings continued, though with many vicissitudes, for many reigns. The twenty-third dynasty consisted of three kings, and the period was one of incessant struggle with Assyrians on the north and Ethiopians on the south. The twenty-fourth dynasty is unknown. The long commotions resulted in the establishment of the Ethiopian kings upon the Egyptian throne. They were Ethiopian only in name, however, being descendants of priests and princes of the Egyptian race, who had taken refuge during the Assyrian domination in the regions watered by the Upper Nile. The Assyrians still ruled by means of petty kings whom they supported in Lower Egypt, while the Ethiopians had sway in Thebes and the country above. Full accounts of this period of intestine commotion have been found in memorial stones at Mount Barkal. These relate principally to the exploits of the kings Piankhi and Miamun Nut. It is needless for any but archæologists to attempt to follow the few and uncertain lights in this dark era. It is perhaps enough to add that after a long period of utter confusion, in which Egyptians, Assyrians, and Ethiopians were constantly in arms, peace came to the distracted country under the benign rule of Psametik I., who was doubly fortunate in preserving his own northern realm and in wedding the heiress of the Ethiopian line, the great-grand-daughter of the king Piankhi and of the beautiful queen Ameniritis.

The splendid alabaster statue of the queen-mother Ameniritis, which was found at Karnak, and now adorns the rooms of the Egyptian Museum at Boulaq, is in this point of view a most important and suggestive memorial of that age. Sweet peace seems to hover about her features; even the flower in her hand suggests her high mission as reconciler of the long feud.

The name Psametik is also of Ethiopian origin, and signifies 'Son of the sun.' His seat was at Saïr in the north. The dynasty so happily begun lasted one hundred and thirty-eight years, when Egypt was once more conquered, B. C. 527, by a Persian army under Cambyses. The rule of the Persians, under six or more kings, lasted one hundred and three years.

From this epoch the monuments are conspicuously silent. There are only isolated inscriptions, containing no records of the victories of each age, but continual songs of woe, which we must read between the lines. They form the dying swan-song of the mighty empire on the Nile.

It is no longer the everlasting stone or monument that makes known to us the unenviable fortune of the land; but it is the inquisitive Greek, who travels through the Nile valley under the protection of the Persians or the kings of his own race, and gathers his information from ignorant interpreters, that becomes henceforth the source of our knowledge.

The monuments of the twenty-sixth dynasty, belonging to the seventh and sixth centuries B. C., are distinguished by a peculiar beauty — one might almost use the word elegance — in which we cannot fail to recognize foreign, that is, Greek, influence. An extreme neatness of manipulation in the drawings and lines, in imitation of the best epochs of art in earlier times, serves for the instant recognition of the work of this age, the fineness of which often reminds us of the performances of a seal-engraver. There rests upon the work, which is executed in the hardest stone with a finish equal to metal-casting, a gentle and almost feminine tenderness, which has impressed upon the imitations of living creatures the stamp of an incredible delicacy both of conception and execution.

It should be mentioned that Darius I. conceived the bold plan of connecting the Red Sea with the

Nile by a canal. The remains of a statue of the king, as well as several memorial stones covered with triplicate cuneiform inscriptions and with Egyptian hieroglyphics, which have been found near the line of the canal (north of Suez), place the fact beyond all doubt. One of the tablets is thus translated:

"Says Darius the king: 'I am a Persian; with (the power of) Persia I conquered Egypt (Mudrâya). I ordered this canal to be dug, from the river called Pirâva (the Nile), which flows in Egypt, to the sea which comes out of Persia.* This canal was afterwards dug there, as I had commanded, and I said, "Go, and destroy half of the canal from Bira† to the coast." For so was my will.'"

According to Strabo's statement, cited by Oppert,‡ Darius left off constructing the canal because some

---

* This seems to apply to the Erythræan Sea, in the wide sense in which the name is used by Herodotus, including what is now called the Arabian Sea, with the Persian Gulf and Red Sea, the latter having also the special name of the Arabian Gulf. — ED.

† May we perhaps understand by Bira the Egyptian Pi-ra, 'the [city of] the Sun,' namely, Heliopolis?

‡ Strabo, xvii., p. 804. Oppert's own words will be found interesting: "We can read through the laconism of this inscription which, allowing for the position in which the king places himself, nevertheless establishes a failure. Darius wished to unite the Nile and the sea by a fresh-water canal; to resume and finish the work which had been attributed first to Sesostris, and which Neco, the son of Psammetichus, had in vain tried to accomplish. But neither was Darius able to bring the work to a successful issue."

had assured him that Egypt lay below the level of the Red Sea, and so the danger was threatened of seeing the whole land laid under water.

Two dynasties followed, the twenty-ninth and thirtieth, at Mendes and Sebennytus, but the records are for the most part silent concerning them. The thirty-first dynasty was Persian, and consisted of three monarchs, whose reigns amounted only to eight years. In the year 332 B. C., Egypt was conquered by Alexander the Great, and with this event the history as written by Dr. Brugsch concludes. The subsequent history is to be found in the classical writers, and in various modern reproductions.

CHAPTER XII.

THE EXODUS AND THE EGYPTIAN MONUMENTS.

A Discourse delivered on the Occasion of the International Congress of Orientalists in London, September 17, 1874. *By* HENRY BRUGSCH-BEY, *Delegate of his Highness Ismaël I., Khedive of Egypt. Translated from the French Original.*

ADVERTISEMENT
TO THE ORIGINAL EDITION.

THE publication of this Memoir, which should have appeared a year ago, has been delayed by the absence of the author, while in official charge of an expedition into the interior of the Libyan Desert, of Egypt, and of Nubia. On returning from this journey, he was able to take advantage of his stay in the eastern part of Lower Egypt, to examine the sites, and to verify the topographical and geographical views, which form the subject of this Memoir.

The author is happy to be able to state, that his new researches have contributed to prove, even to the smallest details, the conclusions which the papyri and the monuments compelled him to form

THE EXODUS OF ISRAEL. 197

with regard to the topographical direction of the Exodus, and to the stations where the Hebrews halted, as related in Holy Scripture. In a special Memoir, which will form a complete chapter of my periodical publication, 'The Bible and the Monuments' (*Bibel und Denkmaeler*), announced several months since, the reader will find a collection of all the materials drawn from the monuments, which have enabled me to re-establish the route of the Jews after their departure from Egypt, and which prove incontestably that the labors of Messrs. Unruh and Schleiden * on the same subject were based on views as near the truth as was then possible.

Notwithstanding the very hostile and sometimes not very Christian attacks which these new views have had to sustain on the part of several orthodox scholars, the author of this discourse ventures to affirm that the number of monumental indications is every day accumulating, and continually furnishing new proofs in favor of our discovery. Any one must certainly be blind who refuses to see the flood of light which the papyri and other Egyptian monuments are throwing upon the venerable records of Holy Scripture; and, above all, there must needs be

* See page 203 of the following Discourse.

a wilful mistaking of the first laws of criticism by those who wish to discover contradictions, which really exist only in the imagination of opponents.

NOTE. — In our translation, we follow Dr. Brugsch's orthography of the proper names, which, in this Memoir, he has adapted to the French language in which it was written, as, for the chief example, in the use of *ou* for the pure *u* used in his German text.
We have not thought it necessary to encumber the pages with Notes referring to all the points already touched on in the History, and here collected into one focus of light thrown on the subject in hand. — ED.

PREFACE.

THE following pages contain the printed report of the Discourse which the delegate of his Highness Ismaël I, Khedive of Egypt, had the honor to deliver on the evening of September 17, 1874, at the International Congress of Orientalists in London.

Although the necessarily restricted limits of time, and the consideration due to an indulgent audience, did not permit him to develop all the details of a question, the solution of which has occupied him through a long course of years, the lively marks of satisfaction with which his hearers were pleased to honor him, and which were echoed by journals held in the highest esteem, impose on him the duty of presenting to the public the contents of this discourse under the form of a Memoir drawn up on the programme of his subject.

The more that his researches and investigations on the Exodus, founded on the study of the monuments, appear to present to the author results which are entirely opposed to the views hitherto adopted with regard to this part of the history of the Hebrews, so much the more does he feel almost compelled to publish the materials which have supplied him with a foundation, and which have imperatively led him to present the departure of the Jews from Egypt in its true light.

Those who are afraid of meeting in these new hypotheses attacks upon the statements of Holy Scripture,—from which may God preserve me,—or the suggestion of doubts relative to the sacred history, may feel completely reassured. Far from lessening the authority and the weight of the Books on which our religion is founded, the results at which the author of this Memoir has arrived— thanks to the authentic indications of the monuments — will serve, on the contrary, as testimonies to establish the supreme veracity of the Sacred Scriptures, and to prove the antiquity of their origin and of their sources.

The author cannot conclude without fulfilling a sacred duty by thanking his august Master, in the name of science, for the numerous efforts which he has generously devoted to the development of historical studies and to the service of the monuments of his country. Having found in the person of our excellent and learned friend and colleague, Mariette Bey, one as devoted as he was qualified by skill and experience to carry out his enlightened ideas, his Highness the Khedive of Egypt has perfectly understood and accomplished the high mission which divine Providence has reserved for him, that of being the regenerator of Egypt, ancient as well as modern. H. B.

THE MEMOIR.

His Highness the Khedive of Egypt, Ismaël Pacha, has granted me the honor of representing his country at the International Congress of Orientalists in London. On this occasion, the enlightened prince, who has rendered so many services to the science I profess, has ordered me to express, in his name, to the illustrious members of the Congress, his most lively sympathy, and his sincere admiration for the invaluable labors with which they have enriched science, in bringing back to life by their researches the remotest past of those happy countries of the East, which were the cradle of humanity and the centres of primitive civilization.

If his Highness has deigned to fix his choice on me as his delegate to London, I owe this distinction less to my humble deserts than to the special character of my latest researches on the subject of the history of the Hebrews in Egypt.

Knowing the lively interest with which the English world follows those discoveries, above all others, which have a bearing upon the venerable records of Holy Scripture, his Highness has charged me to lay before this honorable Congress the most conspicuous results of my studies, founded on the interpretation of the monuments of Egypt.

In thus laying before you a page of the history of the Hebrews in Egypt, I would flatter myself with the hope that I may be able to reward your attention, and thereby justify the high confidence with which his Highness has been pleased to honor me.

I am to speak of the exodus of the Hebrews. But, before entering on my subject, I will take leave to make one observation. I wish to state that my discussion is based, on the one hand, upon the texts of Holy Scripture, in which I have not to change a single iota; on the other hand, upon the Egyptian monumental inscriptions, explained according to the laws of a sound criticism, free from all bias of a fanciful character.

If for almost twenty centuries, as I shall have occasion to prove, the translators and the interpreters of Holy Scripture have wrongly understood and rendered the geographical notions contained in that part of the biblical text which describes the sojourn of the Hebrews in Egypt, the error, most certainly, is not due to the sacred narrative, but to those who, unacquainted with the history and geography of the remote times which were contemporary with the events in the history of the Hebrews in Egypt, have labored to reconstruct, at any cost, the exodus of the Hebrews after the scale of their scanty knowledge, not to say, of their most complete ignorance.

According to Holy Scripture, Moses, after having obtained from the pharaoh of his age permission to lead into the Desert the children of Israel, worn out with their hard servitude in building the two cities of Pitom and Ramses,* started with his people from the city of Ramses,† and arrived successively at the stations of Succoth‡ and Etham.§ At this last en-

---

* Exod. i. 11. Observe that Rameses has already been mentioned *by anticipation*, to mark the locality in which the children of Israel were settled when they came into Egypt: — Gen. xlvii. 11: "And Joseph placed his father and his brethren, and gave them a possession in the land of Egypt, in the best of the land, in the land of Rameses, as Pharaoh had commanded." — ED.

† Exod. xii. 37.   ‡ *Ibid.* and xiii. 20.   § *Ibid.* xiii. 20.

campment he turned,* taking the direction towards Migdol and the sea — observe that there is not here a word about the 'Sea of sea-weed'† (the Red Sea) — opposite to the 'entry of Khiroth,' ‡ over against Baal-zephon. Then the Hebrews passed by way of the 'Sea of sea-weed' (translated by the interpreters 'the Red Sea');§ they remained three days in the Desert without finding water; ‖ arrived at Marah, where the water was bitter; ¶ and at length encamped at Elim, a station with springs of sweet water and a little grove of date-palms.**

The different opinions and different results, in tracing the direction of the march of the Hebrews, are just as many as the scholars who have attempted to reconstruct the route of the Hebrews from the data of Holy Scripture. But all these scholars, except only two (see p. 197), have agreed unanimously that the passage through the Red Sea must be regarded as the most fixed point in their system.

I dare not weary your patience by enumerating

* Exod. xiv. 2.
† 'Mer des Algues,' the translation of the Hebrew ים־סוף 'the sea of *souph*,' which the LXX. always render by ἡ ἐρυθρὰ θάλασσα (as also in the N. T., Acts vii. 36, Heb. xi. 29), except in Judges xi. 16, where they preserve the Hebrew name in the form Σίφ. — ED.
‡ Pi-hahiroth, Exod. xiv. 2.   § Exod. xiii. 18, xv. 22.
‖ *Ibid.* xv. 22. As to the name Shur, see below, p 215.
¶ *Ibid.* xv. 23.   ** *Ibid.* xv. 27.

all the routes reconstructed by these scholars, who had certainly the best intentions, and who lacked only one thing—but that very essential—the necessary knowledge of facts in the geography of ancient Egypt. Their general practice, in order to rediscover the itinerary of the Hebrews, was to resort to the Greek and Roman geographers, who lived more than a thousand years after Moses, and to mark the stations of the Hebrews by the Greek or Latin names belonging to the geography of Egypt under the rule of the Ptolemies or the Cæsars.

If a happy chance had preserved that Manual of the Geography of Egypt, which, according to the texts engraved on the walls of the temple of Edfou, was deposited in the Library of that vast sanctuary of the god Horus, and which bore the title of 'The Book of the Towns situated in Egypt with a Description of all that relates to them,' we should have been relieved from all trouble in rediscovering the localities referred to in Holy Scripture. We should only have had to consult this book, to know of what we might be sure with regard to these biblical names. Unfortunately, this work has perished together with so many other papyri, and science has once more to regret the loss of so important a work of Egyptian antiquity. But even this loss is not irreparable! The monuments and the papyri, espe-

THE EXODUS OF ISRAEL. 205

cially those of the dynasty of the Ramessids, contain thousands of texts and notices of a purely geographical kind, making frequent allusion to topographical positions; besides which, a very considerable number of inscriptions, engraved on the walls of the temples, contain tables more or less extensive, which give us the most exact knowledge of the political divisions of Egypt, and the most complete lists of the departments of that country, accompanied by a host of the most curious details.

Let me lay before you the scattered leaves of the lost book of which I have just spoken. Our purpose is to collect them carefully, to put them together in their relation to each other, to try to fill up the gaps, and finally to make out the list of them.

After having been engaged on this work for twenty years, I have succeeded, at the beginning of this year, in reuniting the *membra disjecta* of the great *Corpus Geographiœ* of Egypt, which is composed, according to the Index of my collections, of a number exceeding three thousand six hundred geographical names. In the work of applying the laws of a sound and calm criticism to these rich materials, without allowing myself to be enticed by an accidental resemblance of form in the foreign proper names, when compared with the Egyptian names, I have undertaken to traverse Egypt through all its quarters, in order to obtain a knowledge of the ancient ground in its modern condition, and to satisfy myself, from my own eye-sight, of the changes which the surface of the soil has undergone in different parts of the country during the course of the past centuries.

Having in this manner accomplished a labor which had the only drawback of being sometimes beyond my strength, but which has never worn out my patience, I have the honor of presenting its results, in the form of a summary, to this honorable Congress, as a tribute of respect and esteem due to the illustrious scholars here assembled. While, for my own part, I experience deep satisfaction at having in some sort reached the goal which I proposed to myself twenty years ago, it would prove, on the other hand, my highest recompense, to learn from your judgment that I have recovered a great part of the lost book of the Geography of Ancient Egypt. The application of the geographical results settled and laid down in this summary, which will form the special subject of the present meeting, will furnish you with a fair test of the importance of these results and of their value to historical science.

Will you permit me to begin my exposition by a remark concerning the general topography of the country which we are about to traverse, in order to discover and follow the traces of the Hebrews during their sojourn in Egypt? All the scholars, who have given attention to this subject, are agreed that this country lay on the eastern side of Lower Egypt, to the east of the ancient Pelusiac branch, which has disappeared from the map of modern Egypt, but the direction of which is clearly indicated by the position of the ruins of several great cities which stood on its banks in ancient times. Beginning from the south of the country in question, the city of Anu, the same which Holy Scripture designates by the name of On, identifies for us the position of the Heliopolite nome of the classic authors.

Next, the mounds of Tell-Bast, near the modern village of Zagazig, enable us to fix the ancient site of the city of Pi-bast, a name which Holy Scripture has rendered by the very exact transcription of Pibeseth,* while the Greeks called it Bubastus. It was the chief city of the ancient Bubastite nome.

Pursuing our course towards the north, the vast mounds, near a modern town called Qous by the Copts and Faqous by the Arabs, remove all doubt as to the site of the ancient city of Phacoussa, Phacoussæ, or Phacoussan, which, according to the Greek accounts, was regarded as the chief city of

* Ezek. xxx. 17.

the Arabian nome. It is the same place to which the monumental lists have given the appellation of Gosem, a name easily recognized in that of 'Guesem of Arabia,' used by the Septuagint version as the geographical translation of the famous Land of Goshen.*

Directly to the north, between the Arabian nome, with its capital Gosem, and the Mediterranean Sea, the monumental lists make known to us a district, the Egyptian name of which, 'the point of the north,' indicates at once its northerly position. The Greek writers call it the Nomos Sethroites, a word which seems to be derived from the appellation Set-ro-hatu, 'the region of the river-mouths,' which the ancient Egyptians applied to this part of their country. While classical antiquity uses the name of Heracleopolis Parva to designate its chief town, the monumental lists cite the same place under the name of 'Pitom,' with the addition, 'in the country of Sukot.' Here we at once see two names of great importance, which occur in Holy Scripture under the same forms, the Pithom and the Succoth of the Hebrews.

Without dwelling, for the moment, on this curious discovery, I pass on to the last district of this region, situate in the neighborhood of the preceding one,

* Gen. xlv. 10; xlvi. 34; xlvii. 4, 6, 27; Exod. viii. 22; ix. 26.

between the Pelusiac and Tanitic branches of the Nile. The Egyptian monuments designate it by a compound name, which signifies 'the beginning of the Eastern country,' in complete agreement with its topographical position. Its chief town is named, sometimes Zoān, sometimes Pi-rāmses, 'the city of Ramses.' Here again we have before us two names, which Holy Scripture has preserved perfectly in the two names, Zoan and Rāmses, of one and the same Egyptian city.

As the new geographical definitions which I have now set forth involve certain necessary consequences, I do not for a moment hesitate to declare that I willingly take upon myself the whole responsibility, as much for the accuracy of the philological part of my statement, as for the precision of the geographical sites which I have brought to your knowledge.

After these remarks, I return to Pitom and Ramses. When you have entered, at Port Saïd, from the Mediterranean into the maritime Canal of Suez, your vessel crosses the middle of a great plain, from one end to the other, before stopping on the south at the station called by the engineers of the canal El-Kantara. But during this transit you must give up all hope of being cheered by the view of those verdant and smiling meadows, those forests of date-palms and mulberry-trees, which give to the interior of Lower Egypt — covered with numerous villages and intersected with thousands of canals — the picturesque character of a real garden of God. This vast plain stretches out from the two sides of the maritime canal, without affording your eye, as it ranges over the vast space to the farthest bounds of the horizon, the least point to rest upon. It is a sea of sand, with an infinite number of islets covered with reeds and thorny plants, garnished with a sort of white efflorescence, which leads us to recognize the presence of salt water. In spite of the blue sky, the angel of death has spread his wings over this vast sad solitude, where the least sign of life seems an event. You but rarely meet with the tents of some poor Bedouins, who have wandered into this desert to seek food for their lean cattle.

But the scene changes from the time when the Nile, in the two months of January and February, has begun to cover the lands of Lower Egypt with its waters. The vast plains of sand disappear beneath the surface of immense lakes. The reeds and rushes, which form large thickets, shoot up wonderfully, and millions of water-birds, ranged along the banks of the lagoons or collected in flocks on the islets of the marsh, are busy fishing, disputing with man the rich prey of the waters. Then come the barks manned by the fishermen of Lake Menzaleh, who, during the two or three winter months, ply their calling vigorously, in order afterwards to sell the 'fassikh' (salted fish) to the inhabitants of the Delta and of Upper Egypt.

Such is the general character of this region, which I have traversed three times at different seasons of the year, in order to become acquainted with the peculiarities of its surface; and such are the impressions which I have brought away from my repeated visits. These are the plains, now half desert, half lagoons and marshes, that correspond to the territory of the ancient district of the Sethroite nome, 'the point of the East,' according to the monuments, the capital of which was called Pi-tom, the city of Pithom of the Bible.

In ancient times this district comprised both banks of the Pelusiac branch of the Delta, and extended on the western side as far as the eastern bank of the Tanitic branch. Marshes and lagoons, with a rich vegetation consisting of rushes and reeds, of the lotus and, above all, the papyrus plant, are met with towards the sea-shore: these are the places called by an Egyptian word, Athu, or by the foreign word Souf, that is, 'the marshes of papyrus' of the Egyptian texts. There were also pools and lakes, called by the Semitic name of Birkata, which reached to the neighborhood of Pitom. The district was traversed in all directions by canals, two of which were near the city of Pelusium; each bearing a special name which recalls the use of a Semitic language spoken by the inhabitants of the district in question. The city of Pithom, identical with that of Heracleopolis Parva, the capital of the Sethroitic nome in the age of the Greeks and Romans, was situate half-way on the great road from Pelusium to Tanis: and this indication, given on the authority of the itineraries, furnishes the sole means of fixing its position towards the frontier of the conterminous district of Tanis.

The Egyptian texts give us evident and incontestable proofs that the whole of this region, which formed the district of the Sethroite nome, was denoted by the name of Suku, or Sukot. The foreign source of this designation is indicated by the monuments, and is proved by its relations with the Hebrew words *sok*, *sukkah*, in the plural *sukkoth*, which bear the primary sense of 'tent.' There is nothing surprising in such an appellation, analogies to which are found in the names Scenæ Mandrorum, Scenæ Veteranorum, Scenæ extra Gerasa, given by the ancients to three places situate in Egypt. In these names, then, the principal word, Scenæ, 'tents,'

THE EXODUS OF ISRAEL. 213

has the same signification as the Semitico-Egyptian word Sukot, which recalls to us the name of Succoth, given in Holy Scripture to the first station of the Hebrews when they had left the city of Ramses. This name of 'tents' takes its origin from the encampments of the Bedouin Arabs, who, with the permission of the pharaohs, had taken up their abode in the vast plains of the country of Succoth, and who, from the most remote periods of Egyptian history, had there preserved the manners, the customs, and the religious beliefs, peculiar to their race, and had spread the use of Semitic words, which were at length adopted officially by the Egyptian authorities and scribes.

Thus it is that the greatest number of the proper names, used on the monuments and in the papyri to denote the towns, villages, and canals of the district of Succoth and of the adjacent nome of Tanis, are explained only by means of the vocabulary of the Semitic languages. Very often the existing Egyptian names are changed in such a manner that the Semitic name contains the exact translation of the meaning of the Egyptian name. In this case the Semites have used the same method that the Greeks and Romans employed, namely, to render the proper names of the geography of Egypt by translation into the corresponding words of their own language. In this process they went so far as to substitute the names of the divinities of classical mythology for those of the gods and divinities of the Egyptian pantheon. Hence it is that the classic authors give us names of cities such as Andron-polis (the 'city of men'), Gynæcon-polis (the 'city of women'), Leonton-polis (the 'city of lions'), Crocodilon-polis, Lycon-polis, Elephantine, that is, the cities of crocodiles, of wolves, of the elephant, &c., which exhibit actual translations of the corresponding Egyptian names. And it is thus, also, that the same authors speak of cities called Dios-polis, Hermo-polis, Helio-polis, Aphrodito-polis — that is to say, the cities of the gods Zeus, Hermes, Helios (the sun), and of the goddess Aphrodité — in order to render into Greek the Egyptian names No-Amon, 'the city of Amon,' Pi-thut, 'the city of Thut,' Pi-tom, 'the city of the sun-god Tom,' Pi Hathor, ' the city of the goddess Hathor.' The Hebrews did just the same: and thus there was, at the entrance of the road leading to Palestine, near the lake Sirbonis, a small fortification, to which, as early as the time of the nineteenth dynasty, the Egyptians gave the name of Anbu, that is, 'the wall' or 'fence,' a name, which the Greeks translated according to their custom, calling it Gerrhon (τὸ Γέῤῥον), or, in the plural, Gerrha (τὰ Γέῤῥα).* The Hebrews likewise rendered the meaning of the Egyptian name by a translation, designating the military post on the Egyptian frontier by the name of Shur, which in their language signifies exactly the same as the word Anbu in Egyptian and the word Gerrhon in Greek, namely, 'the wall.' This Shur is the very place which is mentioned in Holy Scripture, not only as a frontier post between Egypt and Palestine, but also as the place whose name was given to the northern part of the desert on that side of Egypt.

It is in the same manner that the Hebrew word Souph, — whose meaning of 'sea-weed, reeds, papyrus-plant' is certified by the dictionaries of the Hebrew language, and which was used to denote a town situate on the Egyptian frontier, at the opposite end of the great Pharaonic road which led towards the south of the Dead Sea, besides giving its name to the Yam Souph, 'the sea of sea-weed,' — this name, I say, contains simply the translation of the Egyptian word Athu, which again signifies the same as the Hebrew word Souph, that is, 'seaweed, or the papyrus plant,' and which was applied

* There was a Chaldæan town of the same name on the Euphrates, and another in Arabia; and a district Γέῤῥης, or Γέῤῥοι, on the Borysthenes, in European Sarmatia; all in positions where we should expect to find frontier fortresses. — ED.

as a general term to denote all the marshes and lagoons of Lower Egypt, which are characterized by their rich vegetation, consisting of papyrus and of rushes. The Egyptians, on their part, knew so well the meaning of the Hebrew word, that they frequently adopted the foreign name of Souph, instead of the word Athu in their own tongue, to denote not only the name of the City of Weeds, but also the Sea of Weeds, the Yam Souph, which we shall meet with further on.

After these remarks of a philological character, which have appeared to me indispensable for the understanding of my subject, I return to the city of Bitom, the chief place of the region of Sukot, about which the monuments furnish us with some very curious pieces of information. I will begin with the divinity worshipped at Pitom and in the district of Sukot. Although the lists of the nomes, as well as the Egyptian texts, expressly designate the sun-god Tom—the same who had splendid temples at On or Heliopolis—as the tutelar deity of Sukot, they nevertheless add, that the god Tom represents solely the Egyptian type corresponding to the divinity of Bitom, who is called by the name of ānkh, and surnamed 'the great god.' The word ānkh, which is of Egyptian origin, signifies 'life,' or 'he who lives,' 'the Living One.' This is the only case, in the

Egyptian texts, of the occurrence of such a name for a god as seems to exclude the notion of idolatry. And in fact, if we take into consideration the presence of families of the Semitic race, who have resided in Egypt at all periods of her history, — including the nation of the Hebrews, — we cannot refuse to recognize in this divine name the trace of a religious tradition, which has been preserved even in the monumental records of the Egyptians. I dare not decide the question, whether the god 'He who Lives' of the Egyptian text is identical with the Jehovah of the Hebrews. At all events, everything tends to this belief, when we remember that the name of Jehovah contains the same meaning as the Egyptian word ānkh, 'He who lives.' According to the monuments, this god, in whose honor a great feast was celebrated on the 13th day of the second month of summer, was served, not by priests, like the other divinities of the Egyptian pantheon, but by two young girls, sisters, who bore the title of honor of Ur-ti, that is, 'the two queens.' A serpent, to whom the Egyptian texts give the epithet of 'the magnificent, splendid,' was regarded as the living symbol of the god of Pitom. It bore the name of Kereh, that is, 'the smooth;' (compare κερϩε, calvus, גבח, smooth, bald.) And this serpent, again, transports us into the camp of the children of Israel in the wilderness; it recalls to us the brazen serpent of Moses, to which the Hebrews offered the perfumes of incense until the time when king Hezekiah decreed the abolition of this ancient serpent worship.*

The relations of the Hebrews with Pitom and Sukot do not, however, end here.

According to the indications of the monuments, the town of Pitom, the chief place of the district of Sukot, had an appellation which it owed to the presence and existence of its god ānkh, 'He who lives,' or 'the Living One,' and which, in the terms of the Egyptian language, was pronounced p-àa-ānkh, 'the habitation, or the dwelling-place, of the god ānkh.' In conformity with this name, the district of Sukot was otherwise called p-u-nt-pàa-ānkh, 'the district of the dwelling-place of the Living One.' Add to this monumental name the Egyptian word za, the well-known designation of the governor of a city or a district, and you will have the title Za-p-u-nt-p-aà-ānkh, 'the governor of the district of the dwelling-place of the Living One,' which a Greek of the time of the Ptolemies would have rendered by the translation, 'the nomarch of the Sethroite nome.'

And now turn to Holy Scripture: it will inform

---

* Numbers xxi. 9; 2 Kings xviii. 4.

you that the pharaoh of Joseph honored his vizier with the long title of Zaphnatpānéakh, which, letter for letter, answers exactly to the long Egyptian word, the analysis of which I have just laid before you. More than this, when Joseph made himself known to his astonished brethren, he said to them: * "I am Joseph your brother; it is not you that sent me into Egypt, it is God. It is God who established me as privy councillor to Pharaoh, and as lord over all his house." The first title, in Hebrew, is written, Ab lé-Pharaoh, in which the translators, from the LXX. downwards, recognized the Hebrew word Ab, 'father;' but we learn from the Egyptian texts that, far from being Hebrew, the title of Ab en pirāo designates the first minister or officer, who was attached exclusively to the household of the pharaoh. Several of the precious historical papyri of the time of the nineteenth dynasty, now in the British Museum, the texts of which consist of simple letters and communications written by scribes and officers of the court, relate to these Ab en pirāo, these superior officers of the pharaoh, whose high rank is clearly indicated by the respectful style of these scribes of inferior rank.

All these observations, the number of which I

---

* Gen. xlv. 4, 8. We follow Dr. Brugsch's translation, which the reader can, of course, compare with the Authorized Version. — ED.

could easily extend by other examples, will serve to demonstrate, in general, the presence of a foreign race on the soil of Sukot, and, especially, to give incontestable proofs of the close relations between the Egyptians and the Hebrews. By what we may call the international use of words belonging to their languages, the Egyptian texts furnish us with direct proofs which certify the existence of foreign peoples in the district of Pitom.

The Egyptian texts, with the famous papyrus of the British Museum at their head, tell us continually of the Hiru-pitu, or Egyptian officers, who were charged with the oversight of these foreign populations residing in the region of Sukot. These same texts make known to us the Adon (a word entirely Semitic in its origin) or superior chiefs of Sukot, magistrates who served as intermediaries in the relations of the Egyptian authorities with these populations. This service, which was not always of a peaceable character, was supported by a body of police (the Mazaiou), whose commander (the Ser) was chosen from among the great personages of the pharaonic court. The Egyptian garrisons of two fortresses constructed on the frontiers of the nome of Sukot watched the entrance and departure of all foreigners into and out of that territory. The first, called Khetam (that is, the fortress), of

Sukot, was situate near the town of Pelusium. It guarded the entrance into the district of Sukot from the side of Arabia. The other, called by a Semitic name Segor, or Segol, that is, 'the barrier,' of Sukot, prevented foreigners from passing the frontier on the southern side and setting foot on the territory of the district adjacent to Tanis-Ramses. Thus the two forts were placed at the two ends of the great road which traversed the plain of Sukot in the midst of its lakes, marshes, and canals. The description which a Roman author, Pliny, has left us of the nature of the roads of this country, may serve to prove that, as early as the beginning of our era, the great road of the district of Sukot was somewhat like the track of the present day, by which the Bedouins of the country and their families alone are able to travel. As might be easily imagined beforehand, the marshy condition of Sukot scarcely permitted the foundation of towns in the interior of this district. Hence the Egyptian texts, in agreement with the notices of the classic writers, speak only of towns and forts *on the frontier.* Allow me to direct your attention especially to a fortress situate at the east of the nome of Sukot, on the border of the Arabian desert, in the neighborhood of a fresh-water lake, and called by its Semitic name, which was adopted by the

Egyptians, Migdol, that is, 'the tower,' and by its purely Egyptian name, Samout. The site of this place is fixed by the position of Tell-es-Semout, a modern name given to some heaps of ruins, which at once recalls the ancient appellation of Samout. As early as the age of the eighteenth dynasty, about two hundred years before the time of Moses, this place was regarded as the most northern point of Egypt, just as on the southern border the city of Elephantine, or Souan (the Assouan of our time), was considered the most southern point of the country. When king Amenophis IV. summoned all the workmen of the country, from the city of Elephantine to Samout (Migdol), the Egyptian text, which has preserved this information for us, says precisely the same as does the prophet Ezekiel, in predicting to the Egyptians of his time the devastation of their country 'from Migdol as far as Seve (Assouan) on the frontier of the land of Kush.'* When I observe that this Migdol is the only place of that name which I have met with in the (Egyptian) geographical texts, among more than three thousand geographical proper names, the proba-

---

* Ezek. xxix. 10; xxx. 6. In our Authorized Version, as so frequently happens, the *right* translation is given in the *margin*, 'from Migdol to Syene,' the text being wrong, and in fact nonsense: 'from the tower of Syene to the border of Ethiopia' is like saying 'from Berwick to the frontier of Scotland.' — ED.

bility at once follows, that the Migdol of the prophet Ezekiel is not different from the Migdol of the Exodus.

It is time to leave the district of Sukot, and to follow by way of Pitom the ancient road which led to Zoān-Tanis, the capital of the frontier district, a distance of twenty-two Roman miles, according to the ancient itineraries. A sandy plain, as vast as it is dreary, called at this day San in remembrance of the ancient name of Zoān, and covered with gigantic ruins of columns, pillars, sphinxes, stêlæ, and stones of buildings, — all these fragments being cut in the hardest material from the granite of Syene, — shows you the position of that city of Tanis, to which the Egyptian texts and the classic authors are agreed in giving the epithet of 'a great and splendid city of Egypt.' According to the geographical inscriptions, the Egyptians gave to this plain, of which Tanis was the centre, the name of Sokhot Zoān, 'the plain of Zoān,' the origin of which name is traced back as far as the age of Ramses II. The author of the 78th Psalm makes use in two verses (12 and 43) of precisely the same phrase in reminding the Hebrews of his time of the miracles which God wrought before their ancestors 'the children of Israel in Egypt, *in the plain of Zoan.*' This remarkable agreement is not accidental, for the knowledge of the Hebrews concerning all that related to Tanis is proved by the note of an annalist, likewise reported in Holy Scripture, that the city of Hebron was built seven years before the foundation of Zoan.*

If the name of Zoan — which the Egyptians, as well as the Hebrews, gave to this great city, and which means 'a station where beasts of burden are laden before starting on a journey' — is of a purely Semitic origin, two other names, which are likewise given to the same place and are inscribed on the monuments discovered at San, reveal their derivation from the Egyptian language. These are the names of Zor and Pi-rāmses. The first, Zor — sometimes Zorn in the plural — has the meaning of the 'strong' place, or places, which agrees with the nature of the country lying towards the east and defended by a great number of fortifications, of which Tanis was one of the strongest.†

The second appellation, Pi-rāmses, 'the city of Ramses,' dates from the time of the second king of

---

* Numb. xiii. 22. Respecting the probable connection in the origin of the cities, which seems to be implied in this mention of them together, see the *Student's Ancient History of the East*, p. 115.—ED.

† The Egyptian name of *Mazor*, applied to this country, shows us the origin of the Hebrew word *Mazor*, which is given in Holy Scripture to the same region.

that name, the founder of all those edifices whose gigantic ruins still astonish the traveller of our day. This is the new city, built close to the ancient Zor, and so often mentioned in the papyri of the British Museum, at which Ramses II. erected sanctuaries and temples in honor of a circle of divinities, called 'the gods of Ramses.' The king caused himself also to be honored with a religious worship, and the texts of the later age make mention of the 'god-king Ramses, surnamed the very valiant.' I cannot omit to quote the name of the high-priests who presided over the different services of religion in the sanctuaries of Zor-Ramses. According to the Egyptian texts these priests bore the name of Khar-toh, that is, 'the warrior.' The origin of this appellation, which seems strange for persons so peaceful, is satisfactorily explained by the Egyptian myths concerning the divinities of the city of Ramses. But the interest attached to this title arises, not so much from these religious legends, as from the fact that Holy Scripture designates by the same name the priests whom Pharaoh summoned to imitate the miracles wrought by Moses. The interpreters of Holy Scripture are agreed that the name of Khartumim, given in the Bible to the Egyptian magicians, in spite of its Hebrew complexion, is evidently derived from an Egyptian word. And here we have the word Khartot, which supplies us not only with the means of discovering the real meaning of Khartumim, but also with a new proof that the scene of the interviews between Pharaoh and Moses is laid in the city of Zoan-Ramses.

The Egyptian records, especially the papyri, abound in dates relating to the building of the new city and sanctuaries of Ramses, and to the labors in stone and in bricks with which the workmen were overburdened to make them complete their task quickly. These Egyptian documents furnish details so precise and specific on this sort of work, that it is impossible not to recognize in them the most evident connection with the 'hard bondage' and 'rigorous service' of the Hebrews on the occasion of building certain edifices at Pitom and Ramses.* Any one must be blind who refuses to see the light which is beginning to shine into the darkness of thirty centuries, and which enables us to transfer to their true places the events which the good Fathers of the Church — excellent Christians, indeed, but ill acquainted with antiquity — would have confounded till the end of time, had not the monuments of the Khedive and the treasures of the British Museum come in good time to our help.

To alter the position of the city of Ramses, in

* Exod. i. 11, 14.

defiance of the evidences of the Egyptian monuments, would involve the introduction of irreparable confusion into the geographical order of the nomes and cities of Egypt.

It was from this city of Zoan-Ramses that, about the year 1600 before our era, and in the twenty-second year of his glorious reign, the great conqueror, Thutmes III., set out at the head of his army to attack the land of Canaan. It was this city into which, in the fifth year of his reign, Ramses II. made his triumphal entry, after having won his victories over the people of the Khetians, and in which, sixteen years later, the same pharaoh concluded the treaty of peace and alliance with the chief of that people. It was this city whose great plains served as the field for the cavalry and troops of the kings to practise their warlike manœuvres. It was this city, whose harbor was filled with Egyptian and Phœnician vessels, which carried on the commerce between Egypt and Syria. It is this city which the Egyptian texts designate expressly as the end of the proper Egyptian territory and the beginning of that of the foreigner. It is this city, of which an Egyptian poet has left us the beautiful description contained in a papyrus of the British Museum. It is the same city where the Ramessids loved to reside, in order to receive foreign embassies and to give orders to the functionaries of their court. This is the very city where the children of Israel experienced the rigors of a long and oppressive slavery, where Moses wrought his miracles in the presence of the pharaoh of his age; and it was from this same city that the Hebrews set out, to quit the fertile land of Egypt.

We will now follow them, stage by stage.

Travellers by land, who were leaving Ramses to pursue their journey towards the east, had two roads that they might follow. One of these led, in a northeasterly direction, from Ramses to Pelusium; passing half-way through the city of Pitom, situate at an equal distance from Ramses and from Pelusium. This is that bad road, described by Pliny, across the lagoons, the marshes, and a whole system of canals of the region of Sukot. According to what the monuments tell us, this road was not very much frequented. It was used by travellers without baggage, while the pharaohs, accompanied by their horses, chariots, and troops, preferred the great Pharaonic road, the Sikkeh-es-soultanieh of the Orientals.

This last contained four stations, each separated from the next by a day's march. These were Ramses, 'the barrier' of Sukot, Khetam, and Migdol. We already know the names and position of these stations, with the exception of the third, called Khetam. This word Khetam, which the Hebrews have rendered by Etham, has the general sense of 'fortress,' as I have proved before. To distinguish it from other Khetams which existed in Egypt, and especially from the Khetam of the province of Sukot, situate near Pelusium, the Egyptian texts very often add to the word the explanatory remark, 'which is situate in the province of Zor,' that is, of Tanis-Ramses.

There is not the least doubt as to the position of this important place, of which we even possess a drawing shown on a monument of Sethos I. at Karnak. According to this drawing, the strong place of Khetam was situate on both banks of a river (the Pelusiac branch of the Nile), and the two opposite parts of the fortress were joined by a great bridge, a Qanthareh (or Kantara), as it is called in Arabic. At a little distance from these two fortresses, and behind them, is found the inhabited town, called in Egyptian Tabenet. While this name at once recalls the name of Daphnæ (Δάφναι), given by the Greek historian Herodotus * to an

* Herod. ii. 30: where all the three frontier fortresses and their objects are mentioned, viz. on the S., the N.E., and the N.W.: ἐπὶ Ψαμμιτίχου βασιλέος φυλακαὶ κατέστασαν ἔν τε Ἐλεφαντίνῃ πόλι πρὸς Αἰθιόπων καὶ ἐν Δάφνῃσι τῇσι Πηλουσίῃσι ἄλλη δὲ πρὸς Ἀραβίων καὶ Σύρων, καὶ ἐν Μαρέῃ πρὸς Λιβύης ἄλλη.

Egyptian fortress, the following observations will result in furnishing proofs of the greatest certainty for the identification now proposed. Herodotus speaks, in the first place, of Daphnæ, in the plural, in agreement with the existence of the two fortresses according to the Egyptian drawing. He gives them the surname of 'the Pelusian' on account of the position of the fortresses in question, on the two opposite banks of the Pelusiac branch. Herodotus says expressly, that at his day (as in former times) there was in this Pelusian Daphnæ a garrison which guarded the entrance into Egypt on the side of Arabia and Syria. The ruins of these two forts, standing over against one another, still exist in our day; and the name of Tell-Defenneh, which they bear, at once recalls the Egyptian name of Tabenet and the name of Daphnæ mentioned by Herodotus. The remembrance of the bridge, the Qanthareh, which joined the two forts of Khetam-Daphnæ, has been likewise preserved to our time, for the name of Guisr-el-Qanthareh, 'the dike of the bridge,' which is now applied to a place situate a little distance east of Khetam, must be regarded as the last reminiscence of the only passage, which, in ancient times, allowed a traveller to enter Egypt dry-shod from the east.

Having thus re-discovered, by means of their

ancient names and their modern positions, the four geographical points which Holy Scripture calls Ramses, Succoth, Etham, and Migdol, situate at a day's distance from one another, I am quite ready to answer the question, whether the Egyptian texts prove to us the existence of a road which led from Ramses to Migdol, through these intermediate stations of Succoth and Etham. Once more the answer is in the highest degree affirmative.

A happy chance — rather let us say, Divine Providence — has preserved, in one of the papyri of the British Museum, the most precious ⁕memorial of the epoch contemporary with the sojourn of the Israelites in Egypt. This is a simple letter, written, more than thirty centuries before our time, by the hand of an Egyptian scribe, to report his journey from the royal palace at Ramses, which was occasioned by the flight of two domestics.

"Thus (he says) I set out from the hall of the royal palace on the 9th day of the 3d month of summer towards evening, in pursuit of the two domestics. Then I arrived at the barrier of Sukot on the 10th day of the same month. I was informed that they (that is, the two fugitives) had decided to go by the southern route. On the 12th day I arrived at Khetam. There I received news that the grooms who came from the country [the lagoons of Suf, said] that the fugitives had got beyond the region of the Wall to the north of the Migdol of King Seti Meneptah."

If you will substitute, in this precious letter, for the mention of the two domestics the name of Moses and the Hebrews, and put in place of the scribe who pursued the two fugitives the pharaoh in person following the traces of the children of Israel, you will have the exact description of the march of the Hebrews related in Egyptian terms.

Exactly as the Hebrews, according to the biblical narrative, started on the 5th day of the 1st month from the city of Ramses,* so our scribe, on the 9th day of the 11th month of the Egyptian year, quits the palace of Ramses to go in pursuit of the two fugitives.

Exactly as the Hebrews arrive at Succoth on the day following their departure,† so the Egyptian enters Sukot the day after he set out from Ramses.

Exactly as the Hebrews stop at Etham, on the third day from their leaving Ramses,‡ so the Egyptian scribe, on the third day of his journey, arrives at Khetam, where the desert begins.

Exactly as the two fugitives, pursued by the scribe, who dares no longer to continue his route in the desert, had taken the northerly direction towards Migdol and the part called in Egyptian 'the Wall,' in Greek 'Gerrhon,' in the Bible 'Shur,' — all names of the same meaning, — so the Hebrews

* Exod. xii. 37. † *Ibid.* ‡ Exod. xiii. 20.

'turned,' as Holy Scripture says,* to enter on the flats of the lake Sirbonis.

To add a single word to these topographical comparisons would only lessen their value. Truth is simple; it needs no long demonstrations.

According to the indications of the monuments, in agreement with what the classical accounts tell us, the Egyptian road led from Migdol towards the Mediterranean Sea, as far as the Wall of Gerrhon (the Shur of the Bible), situate at the (western) extremity of the lake Sirbonis. This latter, which was well known to the ancients, had again long fallen out of remembrance, and even in the last century a French traveller in Egypt naïvely observed that ' to speak of the lake Sirbon is speaking Greek to the Arabs.'† Divided from the Mediterranean by a long tongue of land which, in ancient times, formed the only road from Egypt to Palestine, this lake, or rather this lagoon, covered with a luxuriant vegetation of reeds and papyrus, but in our days almost entirely dried up, concealed unexpected dangers owing to the nature of its shores and the presence of those deadly abysses of which a classic author has left us the following description: ‡

* Exod. xiv. 2.
† Le Mascrier, *Description de l'Egypte*, 1735, p. 104.
‡ Diodorus, i. 30.

"On the eastern side, Egypt is protected in part by the Nile, in part by the desert and marshy plains known under the name of Gulfs (or Pits, τὰ βάραθρα). For between Cœle-Syria and Egypt there is a lake, of very narrow width, but of a wonderful depth, and extending in length about two hundred stadia (twenty geographical miles), which is called Sirbonis; and it exposes the traveller approaching it unawares to unforeseen dangers. For its basin being very narrow like a riband, and surrounded on all sides by great banks of sand, when south winds blow for some time, a quantity of sand is drifted over it. This sand hides the sheet of water from the sight, and confuses the appearance of the lake with the dry land, so that they are indistinguishable. From which cause many *have been swallowed up with their whole armies* through unacquaintance with the nature of the spot and through having mistaken the road. For as the traveller advances gradually, the sand gives way under his feet, and, as if of malignant purpose, deceives those who have ventured on it, till at length, suspecting what is about to happen, they try to help themselves when there is no longer any means of escaping safe. For a man drawn in by the swamp can neither swim, the movements of his body being hampered by the mud, nor can he get out, there being no solid support to raise himself on. The water and sand being so mixed that the nature of both is changed, the place can neither be forded nor crossed in boats. Thus those who are caught in these places are drawn to the bottom of the abyss, having no resource to help themselves, as the banks of sand sink with them. Such is the nature of these plains, with which the name of gulfs ($\beta\acute{\alpha}\varrho\alpha\theta\varrho\alpha$) agrees perfectly." *

Thus the Hebrews, on approaching this tongue of land in a north-easterly direction, found themselves in face of the gulfs, or, in the language of the Egyptian texts, in face of the Khirot (this is

* In this description and a subsequent passage (see p. 239) Diodorus is generally thought to have exaggerated the fate which befell a part, at least, of the Persian army of Artaxerxes Ochus in B. C. 350; but the discoveries and reasonings of Dr. Brugsch give a far more striking significance to the passage and to Milton's image founded on it (*Paradise Lost*, ii. 592-594):

" A gulf profound as that Serbonian bog
Betwixt *D*amiata and Mount Casius old,
Where armies whole have sunk."

As to the different *manner* of the catastrophe, we may observe that the description of Diodorus throws a new light on the description in Exodus. Pharaoh thought he had caught the Israelites 'entangled' between the sea, the desert, and the bog (Exod. xiv. 2); but when they were led safely through by the guiding pillar of fire, which was turned into darkness for their pursuers, it was the Egyptians that became entangled on the treacherous surface, through which 'their chariots dragged heavily' (verse 25) before the whelming wave borne in from the Mediterranean completed their destruction. — Ed.

the ancient word which applies exactly to the gulfs of weedy lakes), near the cite of Gerrhon. We can now perfectly understand the biblical term Pihakhiroth,* a word which literally signifies 'the entrance to the gulfs,' in agreement with the geographical situation. This indication is finally fixed with precision by another place, named Baal-zephon, for † "The Lord spake unto Moses saying, Speak to the children of Israel, that they turn and encamp before Pihakhiroth, between Migdol and the sea, opposite to (lit. 'in the face of') Baal-zephon; ye shall encamp opposite to it, by the sea."

The name of Baal-zephon, which (as the eminent Egyptologist Mr. Goodwin has discovered) is met with in one of the papyri of the British Museum under its Egyptian orthography, Baali-Zapouna, denotes a divinity whose attribute is not far to seek. According to the extremely curious indications furnished by the Egyptian texts on this point, the god Baal-zephon, the 'Lord of the North,' represented under his Semitic name the Egyptian god Amon, the great bird-catcher who frequents the lagoons, the lord of the northern districts and especially of the marshes, to whom the inscriptions expressly give the title of Lord of the Khirot, that is 'gulfs' of the lagoons of papyrus. The Greeks,

* Exod. xiv. 2. † *Ibid.*

after their manner, compared him with one of their corresponding divine types, and thus it was that the god Amon of the lagoons was represented, from the time of the visits made to this region by the Greeks, under the new form of a 'Zeus Kasios (Casius).' The geographical epithet of Casius, given to this Zeus, is explained by the Semitico-Egyptian name of the region where his temple was built. This is Hazi, or Hazion, that is, 'the land of the asylum,' a name which perfectly suits the position of a sanctuary situate at the most advanced point of the Egyptian frontiers towards the east.

It was on this narrow tongue of land, bounded on the one side by the Mediterranean Sea, on the other by the lagoons of weeds, between the entrance to the Khiroth, or the gulfs, on the west, and the sanctuary of Baal-zephon, on the east, that the great catastrophe took place. I may repeat what I have already said upon this subject in another place.

After the Hebrews, marching on foot, had cleared the flats which extend between the Mediterranean Sea and the lake Sirbonis, a great wave took by surprise the Egyptian cavalry and the captains of the war-chariots, who pursued the Hebrews. Hampered in their movements by their frightened horses and their disordered chariots, these captains and cavaliers suffered what, in the course of history, has occasionally befallen not only simple travellers, but whole armies. True, the miracle then ceases to be a miracle; but, let us avow it with full sincerity, the Providence of God still maintains its place and authority.*

When, in the first century of our era, the geographer Strabo, a thoughtful man and a good observer, was travelling in Egypt, he made the following entry in his journal:

"At the time when I was staying at Alexandria the sea rose so high about Pelusium and Mount Casius that it inundated the land, and made the mountain an island, so that the road, which leads past it to Phœnicia, became practicable for vessels." (Strabo, i. p. 58.)

* Dr. Brugsch has here made a perfectly gratuitous concession, and fallen into the common error of confounding a miracle with a special providence. The essence of the miracle consists in the attestation of the *D*ivine presence with His messenger by the time and circumstances of an act, which may nevertheless be in itself an application of what we call the laws of nature to a particular case. It shows the Creator, whose word established the laws of nature — ('He spake and it was done. He commanded and it stood fast') — repeating the word through his prophet or minister, by which those laws are applied to a special purpose and occasion. Thus here the wind and sea waves are the natural instruments: their use, at the will of God and the signal given by Moses, constitute the miracle, without which all becomes unmeaning. — ED.

The important fact is that the destruction of the Egyptian host is shown to have been brought about by the operation of natural forces. This being established, it does not matter whether theologians call it a miracle, or an instance of divine interposition. — U.

Another event of the same kind is related by an ancient historian. Diodorus, speaking of a campaign of the Persian king Artaxerxes against Egypt, mentions a catastrophe which befell his army in the same place: *

"When the king of Persia," he says, "had gathered all his forces, he led them against Egypt. But coming upon the great lake, about which are the places called the gulfs, he lost a part of his army, because he was unaware of the nature of that region."

Without intending to make the least allusion to the passage of the Hebrews, these authors inform us incidentally of historical facts, which are in perfect agreement with all that the sacred books tell us of the passage of the Hebrews across the sea.

Far from diminishing the value of the sacred records on the subject of the departure of the Hebrews out of Egypt, the Egyptian monuments, on the faith of which we are compelled to change our ideas respecting the passage of the Red Sea — traditions cherished from our infancy — the Egyptian monuments, I say, contribute rather to furnish the most striking proofs of the veracity of the biblical narratives, and thus to reassure weak and sceptical minds of the supreme authority and the authenticity of the sacred books.

* Diodorus, xvi. 46.

If, during the course of eighteen centuries, the interpreters have misunderstood and mistranslated the geographical notions contained in Holy Scripture, the error is certainly not due to the sacred history, but to those who, without knowledge of the history and geography of ancient times, have attempted the task of reconstructing the Exodus of the Hebrews, at any cost, on the level of their own imperfect comprehension.

Permit me still one last word on the sequel of the march of the Hebrews after their passage across the gulfs. The sacred books tell us:* "Then Moses led the Israelites from the sea of weeds, and they went out into the desert of Shur, and having gone three days in the desert, they found no water. From thence they came to Marah, but they could not drink of the waters of Marah, because they were bitter. Wherefore the place was called Marah (bitter). Then they came to Elim, where were twelve wells of water and seventy palm-trees; and they encamped there by the waters." †

All these indications agree — as might have been expected beforehand — with our new views on the route of the Israelites. After reaching the Egyptian fortress near the sanctuary of the god Baalzephon, which stood on one of the heights of Mount Casius, the Hebrews found in front of them the road

* Exod. xv. 22, 23. † Exod. xv. 27.

which led from Egypt to the land of the Philistines. According to the command of God, forbidding them to follow this route,* they turned southwards, and thus came to the desert of Shur. This desert of 'the Wall'—so called from a place named in Egyptian 'the Wall,' and in Greek 'Gerrhon,' a word which likewise signifies 'the Wall,' as I have shown above—lay to the east of the two districts of Pitom and Ramses. There was in this desert a road, but little frequented, towards the Gulf of Suez (as we now call it), a road which the Roman writer has characterized as 'rugged with mountains and wanting in water-springs.' †

The bitter waters, at the place called Marah, are recognized in the Bitter Lakes of the Isthmus of Suez. Elim is the place which the Egyptian monuments designate by the name of Aa-lim or Tent-lim, that is 'the town of fish,' situate near the Gulf of Suez, in a northerly direction.

When the Jews arrived at Elim, the words of Holy Scripture—"But God caused the people to make a circuit by the way of the wilderness, towards the Sea of Weeds" ‡—were definitively accomplished.

---

* Exod. xiii. 17.
† Plin. *H. N.* vi. 33 : 'asperum montibus et inops aquarum.'
‡ Exod. xiii. 18.

To follow the Hebrews, stage by stage, till their arrival at Mount Sinai, is not our present task, nor within the scope of this Conference. I will only say that the Egyptian monuments contain all the materials necessary for the recovery of their route, and for the identification of the Hebrew names of the different stations with their corresponding names in Egyptian.*

* See the mention, in the prefixed 'Advertisement' of the Memoir on this subject in Dr. Brugsch's *Bibel und Denkmaeler.*

APPENDIX.

THE TABLE OF ABYDUS.

List of the Kings, with their Epochs, who ruled in Egypt, from the First Pharaoh, Mena, to the End of the Thirty-first Dynasty.

Their names and order, down to the Pharaoh Ramses II. (about B. C. 1350), are founded on the List of Kings in the Table of Abydus (Nos. 1-77).

The numbers added, to mark their Epochs, refer to the succession of generations assumed in our work; but these, from the year 666 onwards, are superseded by the regnal years actually proved.

First Dynasty: of Thinis.   B. C.
1. Mena, ... 4400
2. Tota, ... 4366
3. Atoth, ... 4333
4. Ata, ... 4300
5. Sapti, ... 4266
6. Mirbapen, ... 4233
7. (Semempses), ... 4200
8. Qebeh, ... 4166

Second Dynasty: of Thinis.
9. Buzau, ... 4133
10. Kakau, ... 4100
11. Bainnuter, ... 4066
12. Utnas, ... 4033
13. Seuta, ... 4000

THIRD DYNASTY: OF MEMPHIS.   B. C.

14. Zazai,	3966
15. Nebka,	3933
16. Toser [sa],	3900
17. Tota,	3866
18. Setes,	3833
19. Noferkara,	3800
20. Senoferu	3766

FOURTH DYNASTY: OF MEMPHIS.

21. Khufu,	3733
22. Ratatf,	3700
23. Khafra,	3666
24. Menkara,	3633
25. Shepseskaf,	3600

FIFTH DYNASTY: OF ELEPHANTINE.

26. Uskaf,	3566
27. Sahura,	3533
28. Keka,	3500
29. Noferfra,	3466
30. Ranuser,	3433
31. Menkauhor,	3400
32. Tatkara,	3366
33. Unas,	3333

SIXTH DYNASTY: OF MEMPHIS.

34. Uskara,	3300
35. Teta,	3266
36. Merira Pepi,	3233
37. Merenra,	3200
38. Noferkara,	3166
39. Merenra Zafemsaf,	3133

SEVENTH AND NINTH DYNASTIES.

40. Nuterkara,	3100
41. Menkara,	3066
42. Noferkara,	3033

APPENDIX 245

B. C.

43. Noferkara Nebi, ... 3000
44. Tatkara Shema, ... 2966
45. Noferkara Khontu, ... 2933
46. Merenhor, ... 2900
47. Senoferka, ... 2866
48. Ranka, ... 2833
49. Noferkara Terel, ... 2800
50. Noferkahor, ... 2766
51. Noferkara Pepiseneb, ... 2733
52. Noferkara Annu, ... 2700
53. . . . kaura, ... 2666
54. Noferkaura, ... 2633
55. Noferkauhor, ... 2600
56. Noferarkara, ... 2566
57. Nebkherra Mentuhotep, ... 2533
58. Sankhkara, ... 2500

TWELFTH *DYNASTY*: OF THEBES.

59. Amenemhat I., ... 2466
60. Usurtasen I., ... 2433
61. Amenemhat II., ... 2400
62. Usurtasen II., ... 2366
63. Usurtasen III., ... 2333
64. Amenemhat III., ... 2300
65. Amenemhat IV., ... 2266
A gap, which comprises more than 500 years, } 2233
and during which the time of the Hyksos- } to
kings falls. In all, five dynasties (XIII.— } 1733
XVII.) } (circ.)

EIGHTEENTH *DYNASTY*: OF THEBES.

66. Aahmes, ... 1700
67. Amenhotep I., ... 1666
68. Thutmes I., ... 1633
69. Thutmes II. . . . . . } 1600
70. Thutmes III., ... }
71. Amenhotep II., ... 1566
72. Thutmes IV., ... 1533
73. Amenhotep III., ... 1500

	B. C.
74. Horemhib,	1466
(One generation of heretic kings),	1433

NINETEENTH DYNASTY: OF THEBES.

75. Ramessu I.,	1400
76. Mineptah I. Seti I.,	1366
77. Miamun I. Ramessu II.,	1333
Mineptah II. Hotephima,	1300.
Seti II. Mineptah III.,	1266
Setnakht Merer Miamun II.,	1233

TWENTIETH DYNASTY: OF THEBES.

Ramessu III. Haq-On,	1200
Ramessu IV.,	
Ramessu VI.,	
Meritum,	1166
Ramessu VII.,	
Ramessu VIII.,	
Ramessu IX.—XII.,	1133

TWENTY-FIRST DYNASTY: OF THEBES AND TANIS.

Hirhor,	1100
Piankhi,	1066
Pinotem I.,	1033
Pisebkhan I.,	1000

TWENTY-SECOND DYNASTY: OF BUBASTUS.

Shashanq I.,	966
Usarkon I.,	933
Takeloth I.,	900
Usarkon II.,	866
Shashanq II.,	833
Takeloth II.,	800

TWENTY-THIRD DYNASTY: OF TANIS AND THEBES.

Usarkon	766

TWENTY-FOURTH DYNASTY: OF SAIS AND MEMPHIS.

Bokenranef,	733

APPENDIX. 247

TWENTY-FIFTH DYNASTY: THE ETHIOPIANS.   B. C.

Shabak,	} 700
Shabatak,	
Taharaqa,	693

TWENTY-SIXTH DYNASTY: OF SAIS.

Psamethik I.,	666
Neku,	612
Psamethik II.,	596
Uahabra,	591
Aahmes,	572
Psamethik III.,	528

TWENTY-SEVENTH DYNASTY: THE PERSIANS.

Cambyses,	527
Darius I.,	521
Xerxes I.,	486
Artaxerxes,	465
Xerxes II.,	425
Sogdianus,	—
Darius II.,	424

TWENTY-EIGHTH DYNASTY.

(Amyrtæus.)

TWENTY-NINTH DYNASTY: OF MENDES.

Naifaurot I.,	399
Hagar,	393
Psamut,	380
Naifaurot II.,	379

THIRTIETH DYNASTY: OF SEBENNYTUS.

Nakhthorib,	378
Zibo,	360
Nahktnebef,	358

APPENDIX.

Thirty-first Dynasty: the Persians. B. C.
Ochus, ... 340
Arses, ... 338
Darius III., ... 336
Conquest of Egypt by Alexander the Great, 332

OBELISKS OF THUTMES III. AT HELIOPOLIS.

(Note to page 139.)

ONE of the obelisks set up by Thutmes III. at Heliopolis has a special interest for English readers. Besides the largest pair mentioned by Dr. Brugsch, now at Constantinople and Rome, a smaller pair were transported to Alexandria under Tiberius, and set up in front of Cæsar's temple, where they obtained the well-known name of 'Cleopatra's Needles.' One of them still stands in its place; the other, after lying prostrate for centuries in the sand, was presented to England by Mehemet Ali Pasha in 1820, as a memorial of the famous Egyptian campaign of 1801. But the intention of transporting it to England was only fulfilled in 1878 by the munificence of the eminent surgeon, Mr. Erasmus Wilson, and the persevering enterprise of Mr. John Dixon, C. E., and it is now erected on the Thames Embankment. Its height is sixty-eight feet five inches (less three and one half inches cut off from the broken end to give the base an even surface). The hieroglyphs on two of its faces express the titles of Thutmes III.; on the other two, Ramses II. has added his own; illustrating Dr. Brugsch's remark on the official pomp, devoid of historical information, which is the usual substance of the inscriptions on Egyptian obelisks. The inscriptions have been translated by Dr. Birch; and a full account of the obelisk, from its cutting out of the quarries at Syene to its adventurous voyage across the Bay of Biscay, has been published by Mr. Erasmus Wilson, and in Mr. Dixon's paper, illustrated with plans, in the 'Proceedings of the Royal United Service Institution.' The very similar inscriptions of Thutmes III. and Ramses II. on the other obelisk, still standing at Alexandria, are translated by M. Chabas in the 'Records of the Past,' Vol. X. pp. 21, foll. — ED.

PASSAGES OF SCRIPTURE TO WHICH REFERENCE IS MADE.

And Joseph was brought down to Egypt: and Potiphar, an officer of Pharaoh, captain of the guard, an Egyptian, bought him of the hands of the Ishmaelites, which had brought him down thither. And the Lord was with Joseph, and he was a prosperous man; and he was in the house of his master the Egyptian. And his master saw that the Lord was with him, and that the Lord made all that he did to prosper in his hand. And Joseph found grace in his sight, and he served him: and he made him overseer over his house, and all that he had he put into his hand. And it came to pass from the time that he had made him overseer in his house, and over all that he had, that the Lord blessed the Egyptian's house for Joseph's sake; and the blessing of the Lord was upon all that he had in the house, and in the field. And he left all that he had in Joseph's hand; and he knew not aught he had, save the bread which he did eat. And Joseph was a goodly person, and well favored. — *Gen.* xxxix. 1-6.

And Pharaoh said unto Joseph, See, I have set thee over all the land of Egypt. And Pharaoh took off his ring from his hand, and put it upon Joseph's hand, and arrayed him in vestures of fine linen, and put a gold chain about his neck; and he made him to ride in the second chariot which he had: and they cried before him, Bow the knee: and he made him ruler over all the land of Egypt And Pharaoh said unto Joseph, I am Pharaoh, and without thee shall no man lift up his hand or foot in all the land of Egypt. And Pharaoh called Joseph's name, Zaphnath-paaneah; and he gave him to wife Asenath the daughter of Poti-pherah, priest of On. And Joseph went out over all the land of Egypt. — *Gen.* xli. 41-45.

They said moreover unto Pharaoh, For to sojourn in the land are we come : for thy servants have no pasture for their flocks; for the famine is sore in the land of Canaan : now therefore, we pray thee, let thy servants dwell in the land of Goshen.

And Joseph placed his father and his brethren, and gave them a possession in the land of Egypt, in the best of the land, in the land of Rameses, as Pharaoh had commanded.

And Israel dwelt in the land of Egypt, in the country of Goshen, and they had possessions therein, and grew, and multiplied exceedingly. — *Gen.* xlvii. 4, 11, 27.

Now there arose up a new king over Egypt which knew not Joseph. And he said unto his people. Behold, the people of the children of Israel are more and mightier than we : Come on, let us deal wisely with them, lest they multiply, and it come to pass, that, when there falleth out any war, they join also unto our enemies, and fight against us, and so get them up out of the land. Therefore they did set over them taskmasters to afflict them with their burdens. And they built for Pharaoh treasure cities, Pithom and Raamses. But the more they afflicted them, the more they multiplied and grew. And they were grieved because of the children of Israel. And the Egyptians made the children of Israel to serve with rigor. And they made their lives bitter with hard bondage, in mortar, and in brick, and in all manner of service in the field: all their service, wherein they made them serve, was with rigor. — *Ex.* i. 8-14.

And the daughter of Pharaoh came down to wash herself at the river; and her maidens walked along by the river's side : and when she saw the ark among the flags, she sent her maid to fetch it. And when she had opened it, she saw the child : and, behold, the babe wept. And she had compassion on him, and said, This is one of the Hebrews' children. Then said his sister to Pharaoh's daughter, Shall I go and call to thee a nurse of the Hebrew women, that she may nurse the child for thee? And Pharaoh's daughter said to her, Go. And the maid went and called the child's mother. And Pharaoh's daughter said unto her, Take this child away and nurse it for me, and I will give thee thy wages. And the woman took the child, and nursed it. And the child grew, and she brought him unto Pharaoh's daughter, and he became her

APPENDIX 251

son. And she called his name Moses: and she said, Because I drew him out of the water. —*Ex.* ii. 5-10.

And the children of Israel journeyed from Rameses to Succoth, about six hundred thousand on foot that were men, beside children. —*Ex.* xii. 37.

And they took their journey from Succoth, and encamped in Etham, in the edge of the wilderness. —*Ex.* xiii. 20.

And the Lord spake unto Moses, saying, Speak unto the children of Israel, that they turn and encamp before Pi-hahiroth, between Migdol and the sea, over against Baal-zephon: before it shall ye encamp by the sea.

But the Egyptians pursued after them, all the horses and chariots of Pharaoh, and his horsemen, and his army, and overtook them encamping by the sea, beside Pi-hahiroth, before Baal-zephon. —*Ex.* xiv. 1, 2, 9.

So Moses brought Israel from the Red Sea, and they went out into the wilderness of Shur; and they went three days in the wilderness, and found no water. And when they came to Marah, they could not drink of the waters of Marah, for they were bitter: therefore the name of it was called Marah.

And they came to Elim, where were twelve wells of water, and threescore and ten palm trees: and they encamped there by the waters. —*Ex.* xv. 22, 23, 27.

NOTES.

THE body of this work was written in German, and the concluding Memoir in French. The translation was begun by the late Henry *D*anby Seymour, F.R.G.S., and was completed by Philip Smith, B.A. Most of the foot-notes are by Dr. Brugsch; those by the latter of the translators are signed "Ed." A few have been added by the editor of the present compilation.

The chief difficulty that presents itself to the English reader is the confusion of names arising from the different modes of representing the ancient symbols of sounds in modern letters. Dr. Brugsch has adopted a mode of spelling which is unusual, and is not uniform. He has followed the German use of letters generally, though in the Memoir his method is often like the French. In his reproduction of Egyptian names, *a* has the broad sound as in father, *e* the sound of *ā*, *i* the sound of *e*, and *o* is generally long. Consonants are used without much system. *K* or *Kh* and *Q* (without the *u* following) appear to be equivalents. *S* has generally the sound of *Sh* at the beginning of a word. The liquids *l* and *r* are interchangeable; so, sometimes, are *u* and *v*. Thus we have Ribu or Libu; Ruten or Luten; Khar, Char, Khal or Chal; Nahar or Nahal; Rutennu or Lutennu; Khetam or Chetam; Boolaq or Boulak; Kheta, Khita, Khiti or Kiti; Avaris, Auaris or Awaris. So, also, Pi-tom, Pithom or Pitum: Serbonis or Sirbonis. The use of Q and *q* is noticeable, as in Qebeh and Saqqarah.

Page 46. *Horus*, a god, fabled as an ancestor of pharaohs, son of Osiris and Isis.

P. 87. *Ramessides*, *Ramesids*, the pharaohs that bore the name of Ramses or Ramessu.

Pp. 97, 98. The note by Dr. Brugsch on the pronunciation of *Khufu* (Shufu, Shoofoo) shows how difficult it is to understand the resemblance of modern to ancient sounds.

P. 117. "*I gained a hand*" means that having killed an enemy he cut off one of his hands as a trophy.

P. 119. *Kush*, Nubia.

P. 133. The title *Zaphnatpaneakh* is translated or "guessed" by one of the principal commentators as "revealer of the secret"!

P. 139. *Scarabæus*, literally a beetle, a favorite form of golden ornament.

P. 154. *Ra* appears to have been the sun-god of the east, or morning; *Tom*, or *Toom*, the god of the west, or the setting sun.

P. 184. Dr. Brugsch had already inserted this document on page 82.

Mineptah was the second title of Seti I.; and his son and successor, who is the only one that wore the name as his leading title, is called sometimes Mineptah I. and sometimes II. The name signifies "the friend of Ptah."

P. 205. *Membra disjecta*, the scattered parts of the body of Egyptian geography.

P. 225. *Khartoh*, in French would have the same sound as *Khartot* on page 226.

P. 228. "The bad road" would of course be impassable at the time of the inundation.

The termination *hotep* signifies servant. The name Amon-hotep (servant of Amon) was called Amunoph by the Greeks, as Aahmes was called Amosis, and Seti, Sethos or Sethosis.

Semites (descendants of Shem), a branch of the human family that includes the Jews, Arabs, and a few other peoples.

Pi and *No* signify a town or city, as Pi-Ramses, No-Amon.

Tell, a mound (Arabic), indicating the site of a ruined city.

Nome (Greek, Nomos), a district.

NOTES. 255

Cartouche, a royal escutcheon, or coat of arms, consisting of symbols arranged in oval form, and graven upon the public works erected in the reign of the pharaoh for the time being. Sometimes a single oval was used; sometimes two or more (or even six) were sculptured. This discovery, made by Champollion, has been of the utmost importance in determining the chronology of Egypt.

Asebi, Cyprus.

Khita, Canaan.

Naharain, Mesopotamia.

The gods of Egypt were many. The chief were

(1) *Amon* (corresponding to Zeus), universally venerated.

(2) *Ptah*, Patah (Former, Creator), worshipped at Memphis for the most part.

(3) *Osiris*, fabled to have been of the human race, afterwards deified, and become the Judge of All.

(4) *Isis*, the wife of Osiris.

(5) *Horus*, son of Osiris and Isis.

(6) *Thut*, scribe of the gods.

(7) *Bast* or *Pasht*, goddess of lust (cat-headed), whose seat was at Bubastus.

A further enumeration is unnecessary here.

The Book of the *Dead*, referred to by Dr. Brugsch, is a manual of morals, observances, and worship. It is of unknown antiquity, but portions of it have been found in the grave-clothes of persons who died before the building of the pyramids. Its circulation was universal among lettered Egyptians, and a number of more or less perfect copies are extant.

In the 125th chapter is described the appearance of the soul before the tribunal of Osiris. Each one of the forty-two inquisitors puts a question to the individual on trial. Some questions refer to matters of local importance and the internal regulations of the kingdom, but as a whole they embrace the moral code. We quote some of the declarations:

" Placer of Spirits, Lord of Truth, is thy name . . .
I have not privily done evil against mankind.

I have not told falsehoods.
I have not done what is hateful to the gods.
I have not murdered.
I have not smitten men privily.
I have not stolen.
I have not been idle.
I have not committed adultery.
I have not corrupted women or men.
I have not polluted myself.
I have not blasphemed a god.
I have not falsified measures.
I have not cheated in the weight of the balance.
I have given food to the hungry, drink to the thirsty, clothes to the naked."

INDEX.

	PAGES
AAHMES	116, 121, 129
Aah-hotep, Queen, her jewels	122
About, Edmond	11
Abraham	13
Abydus, Table of	44, 46
Agriculture	33
Alphabet	10
Amenhotep, architect and sculptor	153
Amenhotep III.	153-156
Amenhotep IV. *See* Khunaten.	
Ameniritis, Queen	192
Amu, the	26, 61, 62
Apopi, King	108
Art	11, 36, 60, 193
Architecture	10, 193
Asia, the birthplace	22
Assyrian conquest	189
Auaris	70, 96, 107
Baal-Zephon	236
Baba, tomb of	128
Beni Hassan, tombs of	61
Book of the Dead	40
Cambyses	192
Cephrenes. *See* Kafra.	
Char, or Chal, the	89, 91
Cheops. *See* Khufu.	
Chetam. *See* Khetam.	
Commentators, ignorance of	204
Darius	194
Delta, the	209 *et seq.*
Egypt, geography of	29, 207
Life in	34
Art	36, 193

INDEX

Egypt, Schools	38
Morals	40
Oppression	41
Chronology	42
Assyrian Conquest of	189
Persian Conquest of	192
Egyptians, their origin	22
Elim	241
Ethiopia	25, 192
Exodus, the	202, 203, 228, 231
Gerrhon	214, 215
Greeks as pupils	15
Their art in Egypt	193
Hebrew poetry, prototype of	142-146, 172
Scriptures	13
Heretic King. *See* Khunaten.	
Herodotus on Lake Sirbonis	234
Hirhor	189
Horemhib,	165
Hyksos, the	93, 95, 97-100, 105, 107, 115, 125
Israelites in Egypt	19
As Laborers	149, 226
Dates of	126
Jehovah, the name	217
Joseph, place in chronology	126, 127, 132
Temptation	134
Honors	137, 219
Josephus	95
Kafra, Khafra	54
Kem, Kemi, Khemi	28
Kheta, the	27
Khetam	69, 220, 229
Khufu	51, 97, 98 (note)
Khunaten	14, 159, 163
Letter-writer, an Egyptian	176
Living One, the	216
Marah	241
Manetho	9, 42, 43, 95, 98
Mariette-Bey	9, 45
Memnon, statues of	154
Memphis	47

INDEX

Mena 10, 42, 47
Menkaura 54
Menzaleh, Lake 67, 93
Merris, Princess 182
Migdol 72, 222
Mineptah I. 85, 86
Mineptah II. 183, 185-188
Mœris, Lake 61
Moses 179

Naval Battle of Aahmes 110
Nimrod 189
Nomes 31
Novel, an Egyptian 134
Nub, King 66, 108, 126

Osiris 70

Patah-hotep, Prince, an author 56
Penta-ur, poem of 172
Pharaoh 48, 49
    The Biblical 183
    Drowning of his host 237
Phœnician gods 79
    People 89, 91, 101
Pi-Ramses. See Zoan.
Pi-tom, Pithom 68
Poem in honor of Thutmes III. 142
Potiphar's wife, story of 134
Prayer of Khunaten 14, 162
Psametik I. 192
Pyramids, the, ... 51-55

Ramses, the town. See Zoan.
Ramses II. the Great 169-172, 178, 181
Ramses III 188
Ra-Sekenen 109
Red Sea, the 239
Reedy Sea, the 233, 241
Rutennu, the 103, 104

Seir 84
Semitic subjects and neighbors . . . . 64 *et seq.*
    Words 77
    Idols 78
    Reckoning of Time 81
    Relations with 123
    In Canaan 140

260　INDEX

Senoferu 49
Sirbonis, Lake, ... 233
Sethroitic nome 69
Seti I. 168
Shashank 189
Shasu, the. (*See also* Semitic neighbors.) 82, 97, 98
Shepherd Kings. *See* Hyksos.
Shur 240
Sphinx the 53
Strabo, his relation 238
Suez Canal of Darius 193
　　　　The modern 209
Sukot, Succoth 68, 212

Taa III. 121
Tanis. *See* Zoan.
Thebes 59
Thutmes III. 139, 142, 150
Tini, Thinis 47
Tombs, historical pictures in 61, 128, 148

Zoan, Zoar, Zor 65, 85, 87, 106, 124, 175, 180, 185, 223, 227

APPENDIX.

Table of Abydus 243-248
Obelisks of Thutmes III. at Heliopolis 248
Passages of Scripture to which reference is made 249-251

NOTES 253-256

www.ingramcontent.com/pod-product-compliance
Lightning Source LLC
Chambersburg PA
CBHW061244230426
43662CB00020B/2420